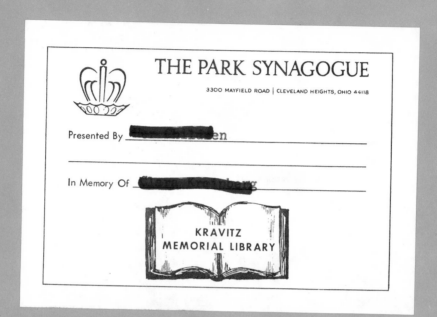

THIS LAND WE LOVE / An affectionate look at Israel

THIS

Text by Nathan Shaham

Drawings by Shemuel Katz

Translated from the Hebrew
by Shlomo Hadari

LAND WE LOVE

An affectionate look at Israel

SABRA BOOKS · NEW YORK

Jericho

ISBN 0-87631-035-8
LIBRARY OF CONGRESS CATALOG CARD NUMBER 79-124127
PRINTED IN ISRAEL BY E. LEWIN-EPSTEIN LTD., BAT YAM
COPYRIGHT © 1970 AMERICAN-ISRAEL PUBLISHING CO., LTD.

Second Printing 1972

This is not a tourist guide, nor is it a collection of reportages.

When a tourist comes to Israel he wants to see places mentioned in the Bible, a kibbutz or two, and the rare and breath-taking landscapes of the wilderness. He goes and sees, he checks what the realities have in common with what he knows from reading and hearsay and study. But a native Israeli who makes the rounds of his country for a second or a third or a fourth time is inevitably bound to meet his own self as child, stripling, or young man rambling and hiking through the same regions when the country was still Palestine or, as we called it, the Land of Israel.

So the tourist will certainly find Holy Places, kibbutz and wilderness in these pages, but all as part of a personal story. For what a man sees in his homeland is not a picture but a narrative.

One of the outstanding Hebrew poets of the Jewish national revival was Saul Tschernichovsky.

One of his poems begins:

Man is no more than the soil of a little country,
Man is no more than the shape of his homeland scene.
Naught save the things his ear absorbed while it was young and fresh,
Naught save the things his eye absorbed ere it had seen too much,
Things that a questing child might meet along the dewy
Path where he stumbled over every tussock . . .

We set out on our way before the Six Day War. We thought we'd roam between the borders and perhaps look over and beyond them also at those childhood vistas that were closed to us. But suddenly, war broke out and the boundaries were open, and so, included in our book are also stories of such places that had belonged to the realm of fairy tales.

rusalem-Jaffa Gate

LAND OF ISRAEL.

Forty-seven years before a Jewish flag caressed the wind on the walls of Jerusalem, a quiet little ceremony took place in the offices of the British Military Governor. The man in charge of the occupied territories handed to Sir Herbert Samuel, High Commissioner on behalf of Her Majesty's Government, a typewritten document constituted of the following words: "Received one Palestine in good condition."

That's British style: that ironic exaggeration of a straight-faced officialese. The ironic pomposity is the alibi of the civilized person whom circumstances coerce into participating in an official event. By making use of it he becomes both spectator and actor. He is the director, the star of the show, and the skeptic audience, all in one.

Sir Herbert, accepting the historic document which transferred the Government in Canaan from the military to a civil authority, signed his name at the bottom and added underneath the abbreviation customarily used in official circles for such receipts: E. &. O. E. (Errors and Omissions Excepted).

The Military reappropriated the receipt, stepped out of the Government

9

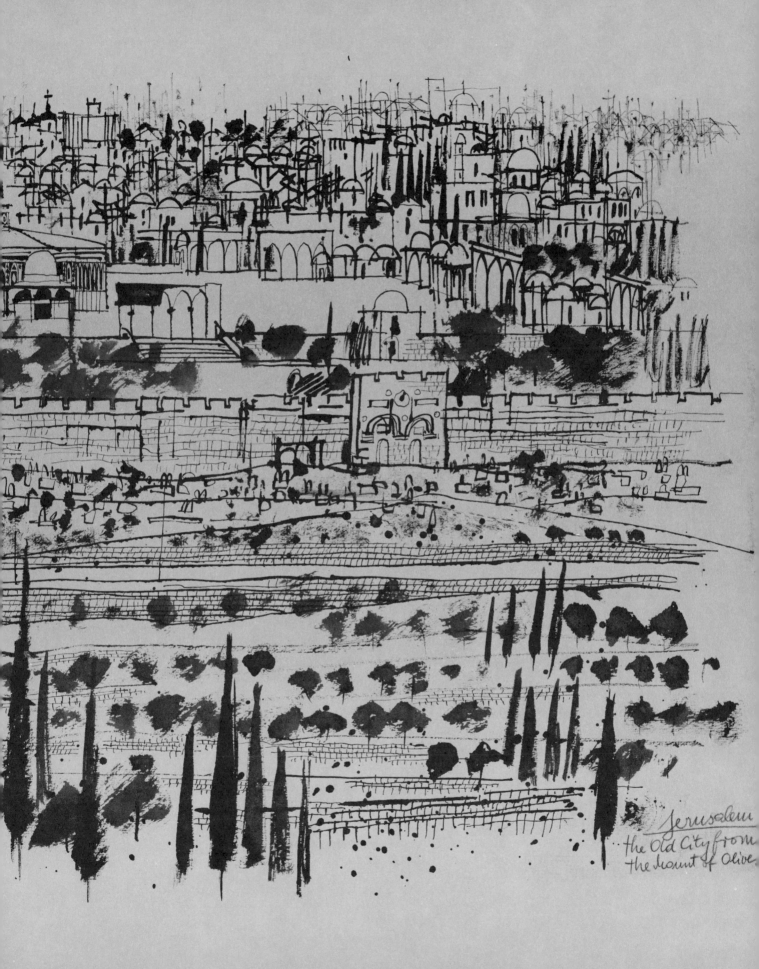

Jerusalem
the Old City from
the Mount of Olives

House, stepped into his waiting car, glanced cursorily at a military-now-turned-civilian guard of honor, and drove away.

"The old order changeth, yielding place to new, . . . lest one good custom should corrupt the world."

Almost fifty years have passed since then. And this Land of Israel, this land that the Arabs called Falastin and that the British consented to name in their documents Palestine, was not once a one, and even less was it in good condition. The only thing which held true were those words hastily scribbled by a sharp-witted London Jew. Errors & Omissions—galore.

HOMELAND HILLS AND VALES.

Children accept the circumstances surrounding their lives as the natural order of things. Those of us born in this land in the twenties accepted as normal facts of life a situation in which life was safe within very sharply defined boundaries, all that lay beyond which stated: Danger. In the dark alleys leading off the end of our tranquil street hate matured and raged, fed by our very existence. Children of our own age, barefooted ragamuffins of a vaguely understood different ancestry hated our bright festive childhood, as if its very happiness was the cause of their anguish.

That place signified in our textbooks as "our Land" was not a place we felt good in. It was neither childhood vistas registering our progress with love, nor a haunted memory of a rag-strewn paradise in which we reigned, a supreme kingdom. For those very plains, that in those days appeared to us large beyond possible exploration, climbing away into a horizon draped

12

Jerusalem.
Temple Mount from the South

the Eilat mountains

about blue mountains, were not open to us. In the blue mountains we were never welcomed guests.

The feeling of security and the sense of identification that a man shares in his childhood's vistas—these we possessed only while we remained within the confines of the Jewish settlement. Anything that took place outside these confines—in the hills, on the boundaries of foreign fields—had never the aspect of a hike in our own homeland; it smacked, rather, of conquest. As if, by overcoming our fears we bought ourselves the right to call the dusty trail meandering between two cactus hedges a landscape of a homeland.

Once, years later, during a trip in Europe, I watched through the coach's window a Swiss peasant's child crossing a snow-covered field, taking a short cut on his way from one village to another. He was walking alone in the blinding plain, his tiny felt-booted feet stomping the marks of his lonely passage extending behind his back.

Suddenly an idea formed in my head: A child in the landscapes of his homeland: All that his eyes can see, his feet may tread. The forest, the field, the vale and the mountains are a picture in the window which slowly unwinds. Like them, too, are the river, the stranger, and the snow which lovingly encloses the tracks of his feet as they break a new path, a one-day wonder on the map of the Federation of Swiss Cantons.

14

EILAT.

I saw Eilat bay for the first time in March 1949. It was the last day of the War of Independence. In my innocence, I truly believed that the war was ended. I was then twenty-three years old and my life for as long as I could remember had to contend with aspects of war. I was a scout, but, like so many of my friends, it was not the enemy we sought in our patrols so much as yet newer vistas and landscapes of our homeland. Often we forgot we were soldiers. Drunk with the view, we regarded ourselves as hikers who incidentally had to bother with a military mission. We were nine persons—a considerable part of the staff of the division that was battering its roadless way through the Negev mountains towards Eilat. Suddenly a window tore for us amongst the sharpened granite crags and through that window, like a blue steel knife, showed a strip of sea.

Without taking the precautions required by military training, as if we were engaged in a pure adventure that disdains the cautious-minded, we made our way via Ras El Nakeb to Um Rashrash. We did not know what was awaiting us there, since that very morning outposts of the Arab legion had still been known to occupy the place, but we had decided that there was no sense in adhering to the dictates of reason. We had just concluded a somewhat comic negotiation with the Egyptian commandant of the border station at Ma'fraque and the enemy appeared to us as no longer very dangerous. At first he believed that Egypt had been taken, and so he greeted us with

15

a white flag. When we had explained to him what was going on, he adopted the mien of a venerable statesman and grandly forbade us to cross the border along the highway. He backed this august pronunciation by lowering a roadblock, which we side-stepped, driving along the wide plain beside it, us and the entire force that followed us, thus leaving roadblock and official dignity intact and getting on our way without a single shot being fired. We were intoxicated with the fantastic sights that unfolded before our eyes from the Negev mountains—one of us, staring from the top of Jebel Abu Aladique at the surrealistic granite cones which, severed at their base, reposed on the edge of the violet-gray granite plain, cried out in true exaltation, "The Valley of the Moon"—and so we saw no sense in travailing with trivialities. Ambush? Mines? Armored outposts? Impossibly irrelevant. Everything posed before our eyes in passionate expectation, a faithful reflection of the palpitating turmoil that was within us all, our very hearts and souls. And there was nought but one single road: Seaward.

THE INK FLAG.

When we got to Eilat, it turned out that we had forgotten something. A flag! We forgot to bring along a flag to fly at the top of a pole, marking the southern border of Israel. But someone was found who improvised—a girl soldier who set out to war provided with clean sheets. A sheet was soon enriched with an ink-drawn David's Shield and two ink stripes—and we had our ink flag.

Nothing would have been more appropriate than our ink flag at the end of that long journey of the War of Independence. It symbolized everything that had been improvised, all that was somehow, anyhow, done with little aid except pride and initiative throughout the war.

We weren't very expert in the business of symbols and rituals, nor did we truly think of it as something deserving much attention. Nevertheless, when

Eilat
1964

Eilat 1950

we reached the last beach, a ceremony was held that contained everything needed to symbolize all that had taken place previously. A sheet smeared with ink stripes, one narrower than the other and both ill-aligned, was flown from the top of a flagpole, without a parade, without the blare of trumpets, lacking anthems and an audience, but filled with humor and a pretense that we were ignorant of the significance of the history that was then being made. For in fact we really did know the meaning of that which fell to our lot, us nine, on behalf of the many who were to gather there within a few hours. Our emotions found outlets in prankish displays.

Promptly after "raising the flag" we piled into one jeep and drove north in the Arava determined to establish our "right to copyright" that we and none others were first to get the flag to Eilat. We then returned with some of the others to make our peace near the improvised flagpole and to share the great honor more equitably. Had it not been for them, who fought it out face-to-face with the enemy in the Arava, our scenic hike might well have had a different, much less happy end.

After the event one knows that such days as that have shaped one's life. Life may yet teach one greater wisdom in dealing with others, but wisdom lacks the etching power of firsthand experience. Thus too the new buildings in Eilat cannot remove from our mind's eye that other vision: the sea, the mud huts, the emptiness, and the feeling of our feet treading Eilat's beach that would henceforth be Jewish.

17

Eilat of today is neither a symbol nor an episode of prideful youth. It is simply another place that people live in. A town of between-seasons tourists, of people crazy about the place, and of optimists who seek to improve their economic situation by benefiting from Arava increments, lower taxes, and the new chances of a new place. For some it is a place in which they seek to plan a life of concrete achievements that accrue together, day by day, bit to bit, material to material possession. To others it is a resort, an experience of forgotten responsibilities, of disregarded claims of daily living, a lazy seeking of a momentary happiness in a hot, humid climate. And some there are for whom it is a temporary stay, at higher earnings, in which one can lead a life of frugality so as to have more to spend in great intoxicated hullabaloos up north, following which, when they are cleaned out, they return once again to sobriety here below. And then again, to toil and save as much as it is possible, to have the more to spend in the north over and over again.

Tourists are shown the port near which it is possible to have water-skiing in winter, airconditioned hotels, fossilized fish, sands in a bottle, minerals, handcrafted African artifacts, and the mountains that rise beyond.

Eilat does have a special character. The temporary inhabitants and those just passing through leave their mark on the life of even the most staid, stable locals. One gets the feeling that the town is forever on the move, like the hot vapors shifting restlessly over the scorching plain. Friends that you had visited a year ago, that you believed had become fixtures, got up and departed between two summers. Perhaps that is why one senses that spirit of adventure that emanates here from everything, even from that worried mother who tries, now that darkness has fallen, to gather in her brood from the street.

A restaurant you enter at random contains this same atmosphere but more so, as if someone has troubled to gather into it, in special anticipation of your presence, everything which might create an "atmosphere": African sailors and an attractive girl tourist from Scandinavia; a wild Arava youth, as careful not to dust his shoes as he is to oil his dust-caked hair; a retired foreman who looks people up and down as if they were job applicants, seated next to a peculiar character who is immersed in a Spanish Catholic paper, and a not-too-young couple staring about them in startled curiosity; an intended drunk as yet on the "one more beer" before he settles down to business; and here, too, is the boy who kicks the ball "like a bomb," twirling car keys on his finger, here to have goodbys of his friends since it is obvious a genius such as his must not be allowed to degenerate in a little place—and all accept it as an inappealable decree of heaven that "there's no room for him in Eilat"; and all apparently are very much strangers yet very well acquainted, waiting patiently for a vacant seat near the noisy,

King Solomon's Pillars, near Eilat

"Alex Morris"
Eilat/1963

crowded table, there to sit and order a huge repast, for "you don't skimp in Eilat," it's the wrong spirit in the wrong place; and no one stares sideways with disguised curiosity at the artist who's busy drawing at a corner nor at his friends who are seated beside him—although they are foreign indeed in this general foreignness that is nevertheless suffused with some of that cloying-to-another that one finds so often in people avid for "aloneness." Eilat is a good place for aloneness of both kinds. One feels that one is among lone wolves—like that bored couple who need company so as to rid themselves of one another—who dearly love an occasional mix-in with the herd.

The restaurant's walls are decorated with drawings by an English sailor who could not afford both a hot meal and enough to drink. Here, too, cosmopolitanism reigns supreme; a collage labeled by neither period nor school. On one wall there is something resembling the bay of Eilat, as represented, however, in the dream landscapes of that artist-sailor, with Poseidon's face sporting the short beard of a Norse sea captain, seen in the bay's water, as crafty as the face of a shipping company's president who has come to hire hands among the natives. Elsewhere, inside a fisherman's net, a Pan with snakelike curls lies in sensuous slumber, his face bearing witness to exhausted lechery, his sleeping form guarded by two gazelles. And over there yet another Pan, this one slightly African, blowing a double-barreled horn and two gourmets feeding at his table.

The restaurant's owner is known to all and sundry by his first name. His face expressing doubtful pride of service, he runs hither and thither, adding to the general din of feeding and the clatter of cutlery which is compounded by a noisy Bach prelude rendered by an orchestra blaring from the wireless —that no one, however, would think to request to tune down, switch off, or switch over to a different station. When you hear the life story of this restaurateur you may believe you have discovered some great principle that underlies the Eilat citizenship that you and your peers shall never be able to grasp. Yet it is a typical Jewish story—the tale of a holocaust fugitive who carries around with him a private holocaust wherever he goes. He came out of the camps with his very skin, having left behind him his family, his property, his hopes, his aspirations, and his very appetite for living. Unlike others who would try to get established on any terms, just so long as they are able to acquire a home and raise a family, he cannot take it. He, having accustomed himself to risk his life for a crumb of bread, to wager all he held dearest in life to win nothing, he could not now reaccustom himself to a life of small change, of adding penny to farthing, of calculations of necessary increments to his old-age pension.

Gambling and card games are his secret passion. He started a business in the north but could not make a living. He went to one southern town and for once in his life was lucky. Things began going well, he had a shop and was putting money in the bank. One night he could resist temptation no longer, got into a riotous game, and on the turn of several cards saw all his earthly possessions and more disappear as a puff of smoke—the savings, the shop, and an additional sum on top which he now had to get from nowhere. So he found his way to Eilat. Here, with his back to the sea, he was compelled to try and lead some sort of a regular life. He didn't have it easy —but not too bad either, for he had managed to start the restaurant, though he is still paying to this day debts acquired on that tempestuous night now years ago. He is already fifty years old and in five years he will have finished paying off the old debts. Worse still, perhaps, he shall have finished paying for the restaurant as well, and once it is his he might risk it and all else he might possess on some lurid night that perhaps is yet to come.

GAZA OF THE STRIP.

Now that the war is over, the road to Sinai is open to desert-lovers: to Gaza, then Rafiach, then El-Arish, then southwards.

Aza of the British Mandate differed from Schem and Hebron. The Jews who lived there weren't numerous enough to breed hatred. The prospering Jewish settlement did not extend to flourishing gardens and intensive planned cultivation that might have roused jealousy. The Jewish population in the whole of the southern part of the country was never so great as to cause worry among the Arab dwellers in Gaza. Events that roused the whole country transpired, it so appeared, away in the distance. The British Army circled it with camps and there was plenty of money for all throughout the war. Palmach squads on reconnaissance missions would enter Gaza for a cool drink in cafés along the main street and mix with the large crowd of Allied soldiers: members of an underground-to-be side by side with the authorities that were to fight it. A lorry loaded with illicit weapons which fouled in Migdal was taken, still loaded, to Gaza for repairs. Even lorries carrying building materials for new Jewish settlements in the Negev entered it free of fear of commotion. The '48–'49 war came and even yet Gaza,

Gaza

Gaza

reluctant to forget her tranquillity, continued, undecided, until it was occupied by the Egyptian Army.

The journey to Gaza is identical to a journey to Rehovot before the latter
drowned in blocks of flats. The coastal strip from Jaffa to Rafiach is of a
piece: dunes abut on orchards; solitary acacia trees; a line of palms straggles
up a sandy hill; the uneven cough of a pump's engine; dogs sprawling in
the shade rousing to chase with fierce barks any passing vehicle.

South of the Erez roadblock one suddenly meets with the old Eretz Israel:
the acacias, the orchards, the wells, the sandy soil eternally absorbing the
slowly pounding hooves of a tired donkey; a veiled Arab woman, carrying
a perspiring water jar on her head; curious children. Near the border one
notes signs of ruin and desolation. Abandoned dogs continue to watch
over abandoned fields, in doubt whether there is sense in barking at passing
armored trucks.

All the way to Gaza reigns a quiet, a Shabatlike tranquillity. A few people
toil here and there at some necessary craft or repairs. Children follow passing
vehicles with their eyes. Adolescents repress their curiosity; as if, by treating
it like something they are accustomed to, they are fighting back in a manner
that might compensate them for their injury. At school they were taught
how to draw the victory; yet defeat, too, lacks the appearance they had
ascribed it in their nightmares. Just people, whose faces are free of hate,
stare at them for a minute, then leave: the enemy, yet human beings all the
same. An enemy minus the apparent trappings of cruel, jeering force. A
man who yet looks somewhat ashamed in that he had come to satisfy his
curiosity by looking at this awful anguish. But then he passes, goes his way,
and bears not the slightest resemblance to the vile monstrosities that fill
the cold textbooks. Perhaps there is here a disappointment in which may
germinate a tiny seed of peace in spite of the surrounding hothouse of flushed
hate . . .

The entrance to Gaza calls to mind a tired but nevertheless apt metaphor:
a busy hive. A hive busy with stingless bees that produce no honey. Men,
women, and children walk hither and thither to a nowhere in four directions.
Bleary, wandering eyes guess what may and may not be permitted. Yesterday
shots were fired in the street, tomorrow a grenade will explode in the market
place, today soldiers are walking around with unloaded arms in the midst
of the bustling crowd. The question forms itself out of the very air: How
long? How far? How?

The army tries not to make things too difficult, and refugees make use of
the general pandemonium to steal from the inhabitants. Merchants open
peepholes and slam their doors. Peddlers stroll in the streets offering merchandise that no one needs. Who needs here pencils—China's contribution
to the war effort of distant strangers. The intellectuals are careful not to

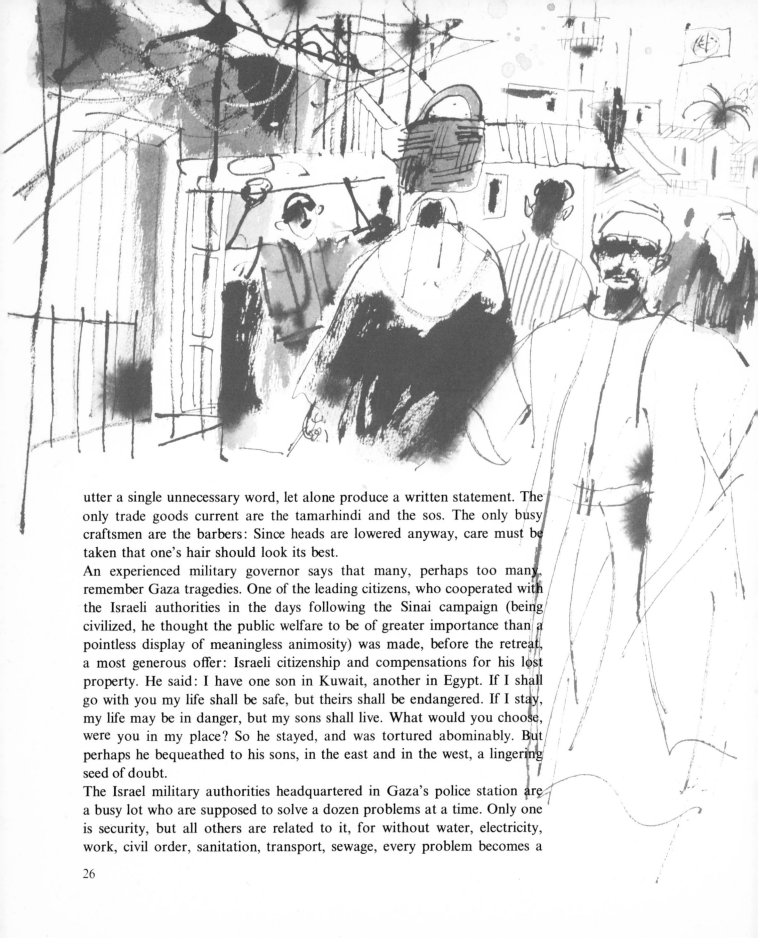

utter a single unnecessary word, let alone produce a written statement. The only trade goods current are the tamarhindi and the sos. The only busy craftsmen are the barbers: Since heads are lowered anyway, care must be taken that one's hair should look its best.

An experienced military governor says that many, perhaps too many, remember Gaza tragedies. One of the leading citizens, who cooperated with the Israeli authorities in the days following the Sinai campaign (being civilized, he thought the public welfare to be of greater importance than a pointless display of meaningless animosity) was made, before the retreat, a most generous offer: Israeli citizenship and compensations for his lost property. He said: I have one son in Kuwait, another in Egypt. If I shall go with you my life shall be safe, but theirs shall be endangered. If I stay, my life may be in danger, but my sons shall live. What would you choose, were you in my place? So he stayed, and was tortured abominably. But perhaps he bequeathed to his sons, in the east and in the west, a lingering seed of doubt.

The Israel military authorities headquartered in Gaza's police station are a busy lot who are supposed to solve a dozen problems at a time. Only one is security, but all others are related to it, for without water, electricity, work, civil order, sanitation, transport, sewage, every problem becomes a

security problem. Enforced idleness will breed hooliganism, hunger, desperation, and revolt.

The Israeli authorities have not come in place of the Egyptian. No one wants today the palatial villa that the Egyptian governor used to occupy, a symbol of his elevated status. Regular officers may improve somewhat their living conditions, or at least bid temporary farewell to their camp-beds—they feel that one cannot run a town in an atmosphere of temporariness. But they do not seek the palaces.

When you enter the police station you feel that nothing has changed since 1948. What the Israeli warrior had been, he still remains. He always has time for old friends, to talk to in the middle of a busy day, to show an ancient synagogue on the beach, to discuss the problems that pester him. "My people need work." ("My people," meaning the men of Gaza who yesterday trained their rifles at his head.) "They need it immediately. It's a problem of organization, security, economics, humanism, whatever you will." He says "humanism" without a preceding hesitation and without a coy glance at the heavens. He is not a professional do-gooder, but a professional with common sense who would sooner boast of personal courage than of personal humanitarianism. The whole business, in his eyes, is rather simple and clear-cut: "While at war, then as at war," and peace immediately to follow. His thoughts are with the future. He is endowed with the great belief that humanism turns enemies into human beings.

27

Khan Yunis

My first sight of the edge of Sinai was from the interior of a covered lorry of the British Army. A red-faced soldier, armed with a submachine gun, stood by the driver, his head sticking above the cabin. He was staring at us with the look of a man trying hard to pretend that he is carrying out a duty of no personal interest. Two other soldiers sat at the back, and through the space between the bayoneted rifle barrels, a beloved land rushed away from us. I had in my hand a card with a hole in it, a bill of lading, as is normally tied by a string to a parcel sent through the post, and on it was all the information that representatives of the authorities required: three numbers: that of the detainee, that of the order of detention, and those of two sub-articles of law slighted by the detainee's refusal to identify himself and to cooperate with his interrogators. The detainees of June 29, 1946—the last attempt of the British to do away with the Jewish Hagana as an alternative military force.

We had already experienced temporary detention in Atlit, interrogation both civilized and otherwise, and we now were on our way to permanent incarceration in Rafiach. Upon arrival at that sorry little town we were greeted by the bored stares of the inhabitants and the gates of a British military camp yawning open their welcome on the very edge of the dunes. Military warehouses in which camp-beds and stretchers were lined close together absorbed us all—the elderly looking forbidding with muted protest, the younger generation looking rather amused.

Detention in Rafiach? It was like winning a lottery. Both the aura of having been a detainee and a long holiday in midsummer. We had plenty of food, both that supplied by the British Army and that supplied by the organized community in Israel, and the company was numerous, varied, and choice. Excepting one hunger strike, which we held more for the principle of the thing, without its hurting us any after our extended guzzling in that barbed-wired resort, we spent our days pleasantly and with remarkably educational effects: So many hours were allocated to public lectures, so many to private studies, and a good deal of time was allowed for sports and just whiling the time away.

We even conducted public assemblies and an active organization of minor underground activities. Although we were placed in four separate camps, each surrounded by double barbed-wire fences and flare mines, we managed very shortly to move from one camp to another, to set up a public committee, an intelligence corps, and contacts with the great outside. The camp was isolated in the dunes, with tiny acacias and a few meager eucalyptuses enclosing it, a parsimonious guard. But we felt neither isolated nor lonely while we lived in such a great congregation of friends. When we left there a few weeks later, we passed through the coastal strip with the bearing of returning heroes. Suntanned, healthy, happy, and filled with a fresh spirit of camaraderie, we presented an absolute contradiction to the spirit of quiet resignation that the administrative detention aimed to induce in us. The only rub: Having returned home when the harvest was well over, we had no few twinges of guilty conscience that we had pleasantly collected unearned glory while our friends were compelled, by our absence, to work all the harder in the harvest.

Rafiach is today the gateway to Sinai, and the outposts of yesterday have returned to function as vineyards and orchards. A south-westerly breeze carries fine dust that in time will cover completely those so innocent-looking communication trenches. That dune, pinched by shrubs, looks exactly like the one where you left the Combine, beyond the barbed-wire fence. The water pipe greets you with a friendly welcome and the shadow, the donkey, and the Beduin follow suit, let alone a friend, an anonymous soldier who, bored to distraction by the little town, is willing to dearly befriend all and sundry. The war is no longer to be found, except in the glances of the inhabitants who, seated in the shade of their huts, roll and count prayer beads in their fingers for days and years.

There is very little shade in that flat, cringing little town. The tallest houses are a bare two stories, and even the minaret needs little height to rise above the houses of the faithful.

The British camp that held us captive no longer exists; a few crumbling roads, a few bare walls still erect in the dunes, forgotten, shapeless, a desolation of something gone to pieces long ago. There is no option but to seek the dear old picture in our memory. Dunes remember nothing. The youngsters—soldiers—must be laughing at us, who've come to seek our twenty-one-year-old footprints in the sand. For dunes do not retain footprints for even an hour. Even that which is built does not persist here. If you abandon it, within days it will start traveling, brick by brick, carried away by passersby. The concrete foundation will eventually be carried away, on a camel.

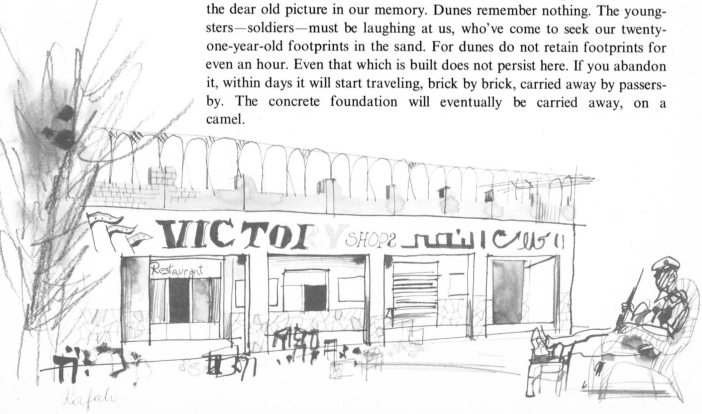

Rafah

Rafah

Donkeys, dogs, and men, too, show no hurry clearing the way for the passing car. Slowly they retreat sideways as if complaining about the intrusion into their normal life stream. At this very minute they were making their ever so slow way to the wall across the road where the shade is now a foot or two across. They intended to stretch there at the side of their friends, draped by a lazy cloud of flies. The car horn appears to have disturbed the eternal tranquillity of absolute idleness. In this desolation of a siesta that lasts from yellow sunrise to purple sunset there appears to be no difference between victory and defeat except in the shape of the letters inscribed on the sides of military vehicles that pass along the road.

EL-ARISH.

Before the settlement of Eretz Israel, when the first pioneers were thinking of going into the wilderness, there were some who thought to make the start in El-Arish. Things turned out otherwise, the plan was put aside, and there's no mark there of a toiling hand to assist in the fight between the vine and the desert wind.

El-Arish

Reaching the palm grove, we paid it a short visit and then camped for a while in its wind-blown shade.

On the crest of a distant dune a Beduin toils, lugging slowly a heavy door on his head. In a moment of lawlessness he thought to enlarge his worldly possessions and now he moves off the road to avoid an undesired encounter with the new order. He can best be likened to a dung beetle that is mistakenly hefting a lump of coal that is of no use to it. What on earth would he do with the door, since he has no house to fix it in? If for firewood, the town is cluttered with empty cases that are not in any sense loot. But then what would a Beduin not do when the forbidden is for a day, miraculously, permitted? Even if it's of no use to him he'll remove an object to a place of hiding. Maybe one day he shall find a house that will lack only a door. So, may luck be with him.

35

Unlike our Beduin friend, urbanites do not exert themselves in vain. Where they can manage without, they do not even bother to put on excessive clothing. Yet the ludicrousness of hate dressed in pajamas! Were it not for the ever present signs of recent destruction, the town would have resembled nothing so much as an oriental farce. A whole town in nightshirts—as varied in style as are the miens of the wearers. The poorest of the poor are dressed in cotton shirts. The not-so-poor sport shirts of synthetic fibers. The middle class wears cotton pajamas and persons of great wealth have nylon pajamas, with a touch of blue at the cuffs of the sleeves and a greenish sunshade to compound their glory from above.

Some of the buildings are truly of the desert and they mingle well in the landscape, but the newer ones are built in the typical Middle-Eastern manner. If you shut one eye at twilight you might think yourself in a Jewish suburb of Jaffa of many years ago. But soon a child in rags will offer to sell you Chinese pencils and thus bring you back with a jerk to the here and now: El-Arish, following the defeat of 1967. A representative of the ministry of agriculture, pacing at your heels, is worried sick: War or no war, vines that have managed to take root in the dunes must not be allowed to shrivel.

THE SUEZ CANAL, SANTA KATERINA, SHARM-EL-SHEIKH.

The scholars are divided amongst themselves: Where is God's mountain? Where was the Torah given to Israel? Opposing factions all quote chapter and verse and bring as witness impressive commentaries. Either way, one truth is soon learnt during even a short journey in the spaces of Sinai: The desert is not an empty desolation. Even if it cannot boast a large population, it is not empty. For where flora, fauna, and men are as scarce, each becomes an entity unto itself: the camel, the Beduin, the broom plant, and the memory-burdened mountain. But as we chose to have here but a snap excursion, our time being short, we cannot allow each sapling and water hole the place it deserves in our book. A man need not be an experienced desert-dweller to understand that a single puddle in the waste arouses in the thirsty traveler a stronger emotion than does a waterfall in the north countries. Unfortunately, however, we cannot accord it here its full due.

For an Israeli not old enough to remember the doings of the British Army in World War II, the Suez Canal was for many years a semifable. He heard a lot about it, but he doubted if he ever would lay his eyes upon it. Therefore, when it appears suddenly to the eyes of the traveler, a narrow course of water of great beauty that puts a stop to the desert and opens the gateway to settled lands, it seems to him that it welcomes him with a wide and friendly grin, offering its cool water to his weary feet. The salvos of cannon

Suez Canal (El Tina)

that greet him from the other bank of the Canal appear to him as something
the mind will not bear. The tranquillity emanating from that aqueduct as
it floats its calm way from sea to sea cannot be grasped as something that can
coexist with cannon shots, strafing airplanes, and the blood-curdling scream
of mortar shells.

Unless he feels like spending his time in an underground bunker, the traveler
hastens south, driving along the beach and the bluer-than-blue sea, visits
the oil drillers' towns, then abandons the beach to get acquainted, following
a bone-rattling journey on a nonexistent road among splintered, heaven-
pointing granite crags, with the Monastery of Santa Katerina.

37

Even if those scholars are right who claim that Moses's mountain, the mountain leaning over Santa Katerina, is not the biblical mountain of God, that mountain deserves, anyway, that God will have paced its promontories. "Divine wrath" is the expression best fit to describe that awesome pile of gigantic rocks that point their stony outcroppings skyward. The very crags appear to be praying, yet in the manner of the ancients: not beseeching in whispers but loudly demanding, in the manner of a race accustomed to treat with gods not knowing how one seeks mercy.

Those who had chosen to build their monastery at the foot of the hills, however, sought to subdue both their bodies and their souls. They would indeed have been hard put to find a better location for the purpose. Distant from

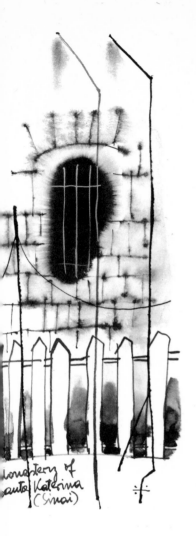

Monastery of Santa Katerina (Sinai)

any settlement, scores of kilometers away from any semblance of civilization, they had locked themselves behind a fortified bastion that until a few years ago did not have in it even a real opening; all truck they had had with that so contracted external world—a meager handful of Beduins, a rare traveler—was conducted via a rope dangled from a lattice near the top of the wall. Within these walls, keeping watch over ancient manuscripts the like of which exist nowhere else in the world, these monks, adherents of the Greek Orthodox faith, maintain a total isolation from all that goes by the name of human life. They appear to have cut themselves off not only from the external world, but from time as well. Here grows a broom plant they say was the very one that was beheld all aflame, yet had not been consumed. There a door of Justinian's day opens onto a corridor at whose end stands a door from the period of the Crusades. Both books and men appear to exist here forever. A mode of living found acceptable so many centuries ago is found just as acceptable today. Only the hierarchy inside was imported from the external human structure. Without a stratified, established order it is impossible for men to live even inside walls in the midst of the wilderness.

The hierarchy of the living is maintained by the dead as well. By the main building—at the side of which there is also a mosque, resplendent in an enviable coexistence—there is the room of the dead. The dead are buried in the monastery's courtyard until their bones are gleaned dry and dehydrated. The remains, each bone separately, the skulls into one pile, the remainder into another, are then chucked in two gruesome piles that have been rising now in the hall of the dry bones for centuries. There is no man who knows what bone belongs to which skull, nor even to which century. Only bishops

in Santa Katerina Monastery

and archbishops were permitted to retain their extremities by them after death. They rest alone, in alcoves closed with a glass wall, each skull beside its own pile of bones, watching over its flock of faithful. Not theirs, that lot, a posthumous pile of anonymity.

So that man shall but find reward for his life of toil.

Sharm-el-Sheikh is a small place with a big name. A stone hut that used to serve the U.N. observers, a small military camp, a boat anchorage and jetty. Had it not served to feed and maintain the guns of Ras Nasrani, a short distance to the northeast, which had been meant to close the straits and sever Israel from Asia and Africa, it is doubtful that it would have enjoyed its widespread fame. For the traveler, anyway, this is the southern border point. One can drive only by jeep to Ras Muhammad, the tip of the peninsula, and from there one can drive only northwards, along either beach, either to the Suez Canal or back to Eilat. Back to the inhabited land, to water that runs in pipes, to electric lights, to the problems that have yet to find a solution. For in the midst of the desert of Sinai, it is possible to truly believe that this tranquil calm that rests on the enormous desert shall persist with us also as we return to the fiery borders of the north.

Sharm-el-Sheikh

On Saturdays and holidays the road teems with trippers just as if there was no war at the borders nor terror in the towns. The average Israeli citizen. it appears, is out seeking the Promised Land. And what may not one find on the road? Shiny new cars side by side with jalopies on parole from garages. It looks as if the very chariots of Pharaoh have been dragged up from the deep. Any vehicle, so long as it's a vehicle. The road stretching southward is an uninterrupted stream of cars, all clamoring, nosing their way along one in the backside of the other.

The homeland may well wonder what has caused this eruption of sudden love that rolls along its highways. A man who seeks to escape his daily worries in nature's splendors may find there, under a nearby tree, his neighbor, his creditor, his grocer, and his income tax official. Not a single sapling in the whole of Judea's desert is without its very own motorized vehicle parked under it for the day. And one may indeed wonder what chases the urbanite into the fields and deserts. Has he discovered of a sudden the beauty hidden in yonder tree? Or is it merely that he's running away from home?

Either way, these determined tourists do see trees, landscapes, and wild flora. And that resin sticking to the new Shabat shirt, one learns to call it by the name of the tree it comes from. Some of the blue mountains that previously constituted a part of the vague faraway acquire names and identities and are added to stores of happy memories. And perhaps, in time even the car owner who now wants only to escape from his home will learn to love nature in a less raucous fashion, will learn to lie by a whispering fountain without drowning its ripples with screams emanating from a clasped transistor to frighten away the birds and the rabbits.

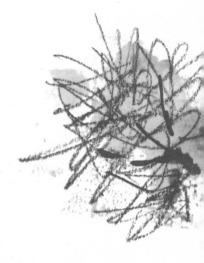

A driver who, seeking a short cut to Arad, followed us on the Lahav-Dvir road wondered upon seeing a family walking on a dune that possessed no "special something" to differentiate it from all the surrounding dunes: "What is there here to see?" The man is in a hurry. He can stop for nothing unless it is something "special." He must get to Ein Gedi and back this very day. Tomorrow, having tired himself out with this compulsory pleasure drive, he must have at least one day of the traditional form of rest—sleep, cold drinks, and canned entertainment—before he goes back to work. So he crosses the border between the Mediterranean and Prairies zones and misses the natural implication of the peaceful coexistence of the thistle and the atriplex side by side with the leatherwood and the immortelle. The white salvia and the dark blue Italian lupleurum are for him mere minor hues in an ill-designed garden—like the carpet he treads at home—for when he goes out for fun he is accustomed to look for color in books and technicolor movies.

42

DESERT'S EDGE.

Spring. And new life, teeming in the rich flora and under the stones. Memories, too, lie here buried like scorpions and termites. One needs but lift a stone and there they are: trips with the youth movement, Palmach patrols, and the awesome journey of war. Nature-lovers dug under stones in those days too, looking for insects, while others worried about mines. Over here a battle took place which you had no part in, except as a spectator, traveling far away on that road over there. Suddenly it was no longer the wide open and a road stretching from one horizon to the other. Those tufts of smoke and dust on top of a lowly hill had become the hub of the world. For some—a few you had known by name, most merely as faces—this place had become that one and very special place for which one is willing to give everything. Nature does not like such memories. It covers everything with a fresh green rug.

Away to the east the desert-lover may be disappointed, for right up to the Arad road extends the chaos of mixed Mediterranean and Prairie flora. And this year, with good seasonal rainfall, wheat and oats of a kind recently imported from North Africa but already successful citizenry, grow such a sea of green on both sides of the dirt track crossing the Beer-Sheva–Hebron road that small cars cannot be seen. Swallows and larks hover in the wheat, while plump partridges heading columns of their offspring stroll about along the track or run lightly in front of the slow-moving cars before disappearing with a clamor among the green stalks, just like the Beduin boys who used to thus accompany in wonder, fear, and animosity any Jewish car that dared pass

"Granite Plain",
southern Negev

through their territory on that stretch of road between Hebron and Beer-Sheva—previous to their becoming citizens of the State of Israel, that is.

But then, they too are no longer what they used to be. They no longer resemble the heroes of the legends told by Lawrence, A'aref el Aaref, and Sir Ronald Storrs. The tents are still here, as are the camels and the smell of smoke. But on either side of the tarmac—that sword that civilization thrusts into the heart of the desert—the plain we remember from our youth as desolation is now sown with grain and various legumes—fodder for the cattle of the grounded Beduin. He no longer resembles that hopping insect that lives here in colonies on the edge of the desert in the meager flora in the wadis, weaving its gossamer threads on the rare green as, wandering from one place to another, it leaves behind cobwebs and dung. He is now a denizen of a locality, building himself a home. And there he is, in person, on a bicycle, law-observing, for he rides along the right, his shirt tail stuffed in his belt, bereft of dagger, horse, and even cartridge belt. Even for a pistol one requires a license nowdays. Hospitality, too, has lost much of its taste when in fifteen minutes the traveler can have a cold drink in Arad; walking strangers are rare indeed. Even the taste for looting is dying for lack of practice and even opportunity: All sheep and cattle are registered at the ministry of agriculture, the grazing pastures are delimited and assigned; roaming necessitates complicated negotiations with the authorities; girl kidnapping is frowned upon by the law that will neither approve of nor countenance such traditions though they be old and respected. Even the glamor of blood vengeance has faded. There's nothing left but to pray for rain, carry the cattle to Beer-Sheva on market days, and check the growth of the bank account.

A NEW TOWN IN THE DESERT.

Arad is a new town. This event in economic life (which is a foregone conclusion: sources of employment gather to them a population; these need services; and since they are thrown together, they have no option but to organize some social life; and as they are many they become a town) is a business for the planner. The hundred and seventy families that live here on an island of concrete, electricity, water, and "cultural activities" are pioneers who got sick and tired of old places that are not amenable to modern designs; or asthmatics who find Arad's climate—so long as the town lacks greenery—better for their complaint than any other; or confirmed thrifters who like to live where it is difficult to spend much money. Whosoever can resist the

bedouin encampment

temptation to buy a car is assured of a future, for he will be rid of the occasional hop to Beer-Sheva where, could he get there, he could amuse himself in the manner of life from which he had escaped. Incidentally, he also assures Arad's future, whether he is a true local patriot or a mere hanger-on-of-pioneers.

This sight, a new town, can be seen only in developing countries. Everything that occurs is but a prelude to something much bigger. Every mote is a potential tree, and every pillar is but the beginning of a palace. A kindergarten is the nucleus from which a university shall grow. First trees and first children grow one beside the other, and young persons who worry themselves each night with "cultural activities," so as not to feel themselves "far out of it," see in their mind's eye a day on which young people like themselves— their sons, those who grew up with the place—shall see nothing special in the fact that they live in Arad; for, indeed, they'll find it hard to comprehend how people can live away from Arad, in the humidity of Tel Aviv or the hot dry climate of the Jordan Valley. The many cars, the radios, the movies, and in time the television—both educational and otherwise—shall bring into their homes the strange and the distant, the foreign and the different from their lives, and the very fact of their existence in Judea's desert shall have nothing in it of pioneering isolation or the feel of the conquest of the wilderness. It will be just a landscape and no more. Just another landscape that can be viewed through the window at dawn and that grows dark at night. A small stretch of country, a piece of homeland landscape for children who see bare hills fringed with meager vegetation as the "natural" face of the earth; all other views—waterfalls, bunched trees in green—being the extraordinary event juxtaposed against the normalcy of the desert.

BEER-SHEVA.

Today it is a planned, modern town. The streets are broad, the buildings are newly designed with painted balconies and folding shutters. There are public parks and an A-class hotel containing a cosmopolitan life in two or three international languages and a wretched Hebrew that wonders what it's doing there in the conditioned air and the perfectly immaculate, entirely impersonal service. The old town has been swallowed up by the new.

A few years before the War of Independence, I saw it for the first time, the Queen of the Negev that used to grow in rainy years and recede in years of drought. It was familiar already, from Arabic folklore and from enchanted tales of enthusiastic predecessors. A real town in the heart of the Negev, in the very middle of the yellow emptiness. We came up from the south, on foot, with parched throats and eyes veiled with exhaustion. We awaited our first faraway glimpse of it as one awaits the revelation of redemption, for we knew that there we should find the end of our hardships. Buses were waiting there to take us to the cool north, to running water, to cold drinks and ice cream, to a hot shower and clean bedding. We had ten days of marching behind us—from Jericho, at the north of the Dead Sea, via Ein Gedi, Masada, Sodom, and the craters near Beer Aslouge (a new Jewish settlement is to go up there soon), to Beer-Sheva.

Patrol scouts among us promised it to us beyond each hill that blocked our field of vision. As we had already promised ourselves relief and riddance of

our pain, we let go a bit and hummed now and then, which we hadn't done before—we had taken care not to stumble, not to whimper nor to squeal (it was better to shut up, for we could get nothing but a squeak of misery out of our throats anyway). The honor of male virility was at stake, not to mention the bidding of the Jewish renaissance which demanded that we make a glorious entrance, our forms proudly erect, a song on our lips and no pitying glances from these hefty Beduins who walk about here thirty kilometers one way then fifty kilometers the other way in the course of their daily business without becoming enthusiastic with themselves and crowding a page in their diaries with a highfaluting flow of verbiage. Since we thought that salvation was near, our will power allowed itself a rest—and that was nearly a catastrophe, as Beer-Sheva refused to reveal itself even beyond the hill that lay beyond the hill, and we were about to decide that it just did not exist or that if it did and was not a legend, then that it was somewhere else, and not on our way at all. We dropped to rest yet once again at the foot of a hill that no longer promised a thing, since much greater than it had borne us but disappointments, when suddenly a front guard, standing beyond the bend of the wadi, called out: "Can see!" The hill was stormed in an instant.

Far away on the plain, angular shapes teemed in the shifting air, standing out from the rounded tendency of the landscape. And tall above them stood the minaret—the pointed finger of fate.

We hid the weapons by the walls of the wadi, in a previously prepared hiding place—there to await the use of another company that would march down from here to the Dead Sea and finally down to Beit Haarava—and out we set to cross the plain leading to Beer-Sheva. But we still had some disappointments to live through. It appeared as if the town moved and shifted ahead of us, like the biblical pillars of fire and smoke. But suddenly it cleared, brightened, and was very near. And then, soon, it was a clamor of camels and the wondering eyes of Beduin boys who worried whether they ought or ought not to throw stones at us, and a colorful market like Jaffa's but without Jaffa's smells, and the suspicious staring of the British policeman, gorgeously white in a cork helmet, with a sunfired nose, and looking like a strange bird with his two red thighs peering from between the short broad pants and long khaki socks that had a pipe stuck in them.

At times, when you return once more to a place visited long before, you try to remember first impressions and your eyes seek those details that had once created a mood. In Beer-Sheva this is not possible. It's like visiting a theatre after the audience has gone, when even the actors have retired to their chambers: everything is there—the material, the form, the boards and cloth—but the magic is gone. For, the second time I visited Beer-Sheva was on the day it was taken in war.

In kitchens on that day, meals were still cooling while the diners were then

49

running away. In the post office gleamed fresh the postmark on a stamp of
Palestine bearing Farouk's image that was about to be sent to Egypt; hair-
dressers' shops still reeked of fresh barbers' oil.

Dead bodies were still strewn by the wayside.

But already it was clear that as of then, things were about to change. There
was no need to use the cliché of a "Hebrew Beer-Sheva," for matters devel-
oped very fast. Partners to our childhood games, young men all, nearly
boys, laid down orders after due deliberation. Military policemen were already locking up yawning stores and looted shops. The Engineering Corps
was clearing away the rubble. Civil authorities soon came to replace martial
law. Almost it was as if the new settlers had stood waiting at the town's
gates.

It wasn't many months before again the town was settled. I remember the return of the Beduins. I attended a great feast the military authorities held in honor of the elders of the tribes that swore allegiance to the State of Israel. It was held in a huge tent on the town's outskirts. On one side sat boys, on the other, regal elders. Everything went along with maximum deliberation and formality in accordance with the ancient manners of the elders in the congregation. The youthful victors who habitually made light of all rituals had suddenly switched around and had taken it upon themselves in good grace to behave in accordance with the social dictates of the defeated. The party was held in their spirit and the talk went according to their fashion: a sad victory of the defeated who knew how to surrender while paying court to their own respect and honor. I still keep by me a souvenir of that meeting, a hooked knife inlaid with colored stones I received from an aged sheik who, when the Sultan Abdul Aziz ascended to the throne shortly before Moses Montefiore's visit to Israel, already milked his father's goats in the Negev mountains; and neither the Turks nor the British had managed to change his habits.

Of course, this is perhaps but a figment of my imagination, but a look he gave me when I received the present from his hands had nothing in it of enmity, as if yesterday was taking off his sword and saying to the today, "Take it, and be gone on your way." Small, wise eyes smiled at me from under eyebrows white as the snow he had never seen. I had nothing to give him, no present to give in return, for barring the pistol I wore, and my clothes, I had virtually nothing in my possession.

ISHITES AT THE FOOTHILLS OF MASADA.

In the spring of 1947 when a Beduin, one of the most miserable of the Gawarna, set out to find a lost goat in the vicinity of mount Qumeran, there moved through that region the last presummer march of the Palmach. The Qumeran scrolls were still secure in their jars in a dark cave. We could "settle" the Ishites where we fancied, at any crack of rock that faced the Dead Sea. Any place that saw the lethal blue glitter beyond the arid yellow was found worthy of the Ishite dwelling—the Ishites were allies. By Ein Fashcha or Ein Taniba, or beside the tiny pool at Ein Gedi—we always selected for our allies a life of pleasant plenty—we would take out a copy of Josephus Flavius—Yoseph ben Matityahu. We were still divided whether he had been a traitor or a historian who foresaw the future and who therefore has call on our gratitude for having supplied us with the missing link. Either way, he did not deserve oblivion. So we'd read our tired friends, while they dipped sore feet in chill water, chapters of the Ishites.

Kibbutz members—a majority in the Palmach—felt at home with Josephus's description of: "... They had neither the shame of poverty nor the pride of wealth amongst them. They wear neither clothes nor new sandals before the old are torn or worn away with use. They neither buy from, nor sell anything to one another. ..."

Allies. Near yet distant brothers, as they had been called by a philosopher among us. A people with a message whose revelation was detained but not lost from the world, as if it was sealed here, in that parsimonious, salt-burned soil, as a challenge to those who do not negate life but who understand hints given them by the nature of the land: Free are those who shall be ready and willing to extract bread from *this* soil. We would remember with envy our friends from Kibbutz Beit Haarava, in whose dining room we danced but yesterday. They treated hospitality in the fashion of the desert people: While we congratulate ourselves for our intent of pioneering, they cleanse the soil of salt, are pioneers of pioneers, Ishites of our times, who say a big yes to life, but without the "shame of poverty" and the "pride of wealth." Some of us—those whose book-learning confined itself to narrow sufficiency —were content with being of the Palmach and stamping with a massive boot the desert and any who would stand in our way. They had no interest in past adventures, especially such as smacked of scholarship and erudition; but then if it was obligatory to pay heed to a few chapters of propaganda, they did so with as good a grace as possible; so long as the feet were immersed in water they did not mind hearing some verses anyway... They paid close attention also to what the writings implied: "... and they were zealously diligent in studying all the early books and most especially those books that promised advantage to their souls and their bodies." These enthusiastically skeptic youth would discover themselves in the ancient manuscripts. Indeed, what with platoon training, company drill, "removal" of immigrants, illegal procurement of weapons, and exhausting marches, very little time was available for books and learning. So we tended to avoid anything that did not directly bring advantage to soul and body. But this abstention was never a principle; it was born of the nature of the land and of the withdrawal from a life subjected to Roman fashions: baths, theatres, a life of leisure in which permanent values dissolve and disappear as lumps of sugar in boiling water.

The Jewish hermit experience was not foreign to our nature. Our very marches in the desert were in such a spirit. Ten solid days of exhausting march, the straps of our packs tearing into our flesh, a conquering army that leaves behind it only footprints in the sand, we'd walk in the desert, year after year, like pilgrims. We were very ordinary men who made an offering of our agony toward the settlement of the land in a place where real life settlement was impossible beyond question.

Wadi Kelet

A DIP IN THE JORDAN.

Today one can drive right up to the monasteries of Wadi Kelet. In Ma'ates, where, by Christian tradition, John the Baptist had baptized Jesus the miracle worker, there are awnings for picnics and the road reaches right up to the very steps that lead to the place of baptism. The Ishites have meanwhile acquired their permanent dwelling in the Ruins of Qumeran. Civilization has reached them too; now both Arabs and Jews carve their names, in two languages, on every historical site.

And we too, it seems, are no longer as we were. Monks and priests are for us no longer something inexplicable. Armed with the wicked tools of psycho-

Jordan River
near El Ma'ates

analysis we eat to our hearts' delight in the shade of eucalyptuses by the Jordan, not far from Kasr-el Yahud, wash our food down with cold beer, and watch the monks toiling in the adjacent orchard as the thin-surfeited watch the hungry-fat suffering the rigors of a diet he forces upon himself. The multitudes of Israel scramble along roads that but yesterday were sealed-off territories and provide an enthusiastic audience to this spectacle of Christian solitude that can no longer find its peace. The road murders the desert. And the Government Tourists' Bureaus, first of the Hashemite Kingdom, then of Israel, put an end to the seclusion from the company of men. These hermits are no more secluded from the congregation than is any simple misanthrope who locks himself behind a stout wooden door in a busy street in populous London or Tokyo. The hermits, just like the Gawarna Beduins, are no longer a rare sight. One Beduin here has realized his life was a spectacle—his tent, his camel, and the veiled woman. A large sign requested foreign tourists to leave "beer money." He is a part of a different culture. It might not be surprising if the hermits, too, should adopt the bottomless source of income of a growing tourism. They might sell tickets to a spectacle of seclusion and present their indifference as a star-turn of a show. But perhaps I am mistaken, and when the iron gates of the monasteries by the Jordan shall open, no one shall care to look inside them. Unless shut, they shall hold no interest. Indifference to other people's lives is to be found in the busiest cities; why seek it out in the plains of Jericho?

In that very place where some twenty years ago I walked with a friend who wanted to enter the meditation chamber of a silent hermit—who opened the door for us and left and would not return until we departed—there stands now an awning, erected to provide shade for the first and last visit of a group of V.I.P.s. Today the place is a picnic ground for a multitude of poor in faith. Multitudes go down to wash their hands and faces, yet return unrepentant. Such, too, were the circumstances under the tutelage of the Kingdom of Jordan. In witness, one man of faith, who thereby acquired the right to carve verses in stone in a holy place, carved there his musings in English and German. Perhaps it was he who had built the awning so he could have his say, a dirge to the diminution of faith: "Where Jesus was baptized a man must make obeisance in repentance. Many there are who come but to satisfy their curiosity, nor do they feel any exultation and inner joy. But the Son of God, in his patience and mercy, shall lift his eyes from the splendid heights of his seat, awaiting the day in which those who foresook the way shall kneel on the bank of the Jordan and in tears shall wash away their sins."

Soldiers, camping for a time in the shade of that awning, feel, it seems, some real joy of soul not due to any thoughts of repentance, however. They kneel by the Jordan and cool their baked faces. It's hot, and yet there's still so much to be done.

55

The tradition begun in the youth movements of pilgrimage to Masada was adopted by the Palmach. What the youth movement called "trip" got in the Palmach a more professional name—"march." In fact there was little difference between them. One year you marched in a long column of friends in the movement. The second year you were marched in an anonymous army, constituted largely of very much the same friends of old. The third year you marched at the head of the column as an armed scout the Palmach provided for protection to the youth movement—the training ground for Palmach reserves.

Sometimes we started out from Beer Aslouge and ended in Beit Haarava, and other times, the other way around. The Southern companies used to cross the desert along its breadth. The first day of such a march would stretch out for over thirty-six hours, for the Mount Hebron district wasn't a good place to get caught carrying arms in daylight. There was a British officer there, who had adopted the local hatreds and who rarely missed a chance to try and get hold of Jewish weapons. We would walk in a forced march, by day along the mountain slopes, by night in Mount Hebron, and until we were sufficiently far into the desert we would not allow ourselves a proper rest. And as there is no rest except next to water, we would not stop until we found some well.

Along the Beer Aslouge route—via both craters, up the Scorpion's Path, Sodom, Masada, Ein Gedi, Ein Tariba, Ein Fashcha, Kalia, and Beit Haarava —the problems of securing our "secret and precious" weapons were less severe. Since the whole march took place in the wilderness, there was no need to march a day and a night and a day without a break merely so that our weapons wouldn't be "tanned by a stranger's eyes," in the words of one of the beautiful songs of those days. Our weapons! A modern reader might imagine a Palmach company marching armed to the teeth just to spite the British authorities who raked kibbutz yards with mine indicators, sought a pair of rifles packed in grease or a pistol bereft of an official license. Heady visions! When we say an "armed company" we mean that it included a platoon that hid among its effects, whether in its members' clothing or in a double-bottomed water bottle, four or five pistols. A really reckless company commander might hide a Mauser with a wooden butt; these were considered tactical long range weapons. Later on we were able to secretly embrace dismembered and properly camouflaged parts of submachine guns.

The company as a body was armed with thin hard wooden staffs for hand-to-hand combat. Secure in our might, enchanted with the unlimited possibilities pregnant in the firepower of our firearms, we were ready to welcome any provocation of valorous Beduins who might wish to acquire our watches

and the sticky halvah that dripped its fat in secret on the Shabat shirt in our packs, the Shabat shirt reserved for the big party by friendly fires that shot to the heavens incandescent stars, years-old songs, and ten-day-old reminiscences.

Some companies did have the luck. A Beduin attack did not fail to materialize. They spread out on the mountain, protecting lives and property, and lay for long hours, each behind some cover, the murderous sun beating down on them while their friends, the happy minority, would answer the fire of rifles with unpretentious crackles emitted from the short barrels of pistols even shorter on ammunition, a clarion call of a renaissance. While we simply practiced, they gained some real "combat experience."

Far be it from me to make light of that combat experience. What was borne in that womb had wrought all the rest: the resourcefulness, the audacity, the stratagems and all that was made use of later when the need arose. Resourcefulness is resourcefulness irrespective of the degree of might it must cope with. For, following a futile fire exchange—the Beduins on the mountains beyond pistol range, and our good friends in the valley, target practice to young herdsmen—the order was given to charge! And two pistolleros, advancing in battle leaps up the face of the mountain, would chase away the valorous Beduins. The latter must have been certain that no one would attack unless he had some very real cover, and so they feared a trap and fled.

The purpose of these marches, however, was not to apply military book-learning. If a chance came by, the most was made of it. But the general lot simply trudged, taught themselves to exact the better from the worse, to extract some deep mysterious pleasure from the ability to overcome pain. They knew they were marching to Masada, and that all it entailed was simply a necessary evil inasmuch as Masada was stuck somewhere above the Dead Sea, far from any settlement and habitation.

The company parade at the foothills of Masada was the crowning glory of the whole march. There we permitted ourselves the niceties of ritual, the company commander would wrap himself in glory and even deliver a short speech—something that must have given him not a few pangs and so aided him in disregarding his private agony. Readers would stand on crags and provoke the echoes that rolled back at them from the canyons: "Into thy portals, Masada, I have come, a fugitive . . ." No one listened to the words. There was an unearthly magic in that music of sound rolling among boulders, in that feeling of absolute seclusion from the external world, in the complete independence of a secluded group of youngsters, in the right to carry arms in the open.

In the days that Rommel's tanks exercised in the open plains of El Alamein, last-ditch battles in the Judea desert were by no means an empty platitude. Just one more British failure would have brought to end all the hopes of

Israel. But we caressed the cold metal of pistols with sun-scorched hands, imbued with a fabulous sense of our might. Having succeeded thus far, having overcome all the obstacles, we were really certain that "Again Masada shall not fall." The feeling of eternity of youth!

The clever among us knew that the great march was not a reconnaissance exercise, and that there was certainly no need to know so well so many of the markings on the map, for a real desert war is fought over axes of movement and water sources. They knew that from the viewpoint of a professional soldier our agonizing rituals were a form of animistic worship. Nevertheless they marched along and kept their doubts to themselves. And then they returned to march again, like men who knew their way with desert paths. And later still, when they were as good at map reading as any professional, they aspired to a yet higher level—that of the Beduin, who does not need any maps.

Perhaps there was in the first days of such marches a challenge to a manhood that does not retire from obstacles. But on the fourth and fifth march a man no longer asks himself whether he can do it. So that march acquired another role. It was not defined as such by many, but it was such by its very nature: a declaration of belonging. As if this tradition claimed for us our right to walk in safety in our homeland. Everywhere. Both where it is out of bounds on purpose and where it is out of bounds by reasons of its wild nature, so different for our cool life shaded and protected by trees and a home.

So it is by no means impossible that within some of us a desire had begun to stir and grow: to adopt as a personal fate the wild, cruel, scorching, arid nature of the homeland. We threw ourselves into the desert so as to make it, too, ours.

A love was born of its own to this land that does not give of itself freely or easily. That secrets its fulsomeness and covers its wells; that demands sacrifices so as to be sure of your love. And when you fell faint on the green edge of a water hole, and blessed in your heart that nomadic culture that consecrates water, you felt of a sudden that those ancient manuscripts were indeed the story of your life.

AGAIN MASADA.

To Masada in an army helicopter, fifty minutes from Sdeh Dov in Tel Aviv to the top of Masada. An oath-of-fealty ceremony of Armored Corps' recruits. The flight, low and "trackless," is, therefore, all the more a reconstruction of that other march, skipping over the hills from here to there in a straight line, a waking dream that enfolds in a flash of speed events that unfolded slowly, like an enamored youth who, lying on his bed with open eyes, sees things that have transpired, one small detail following another down to the

58

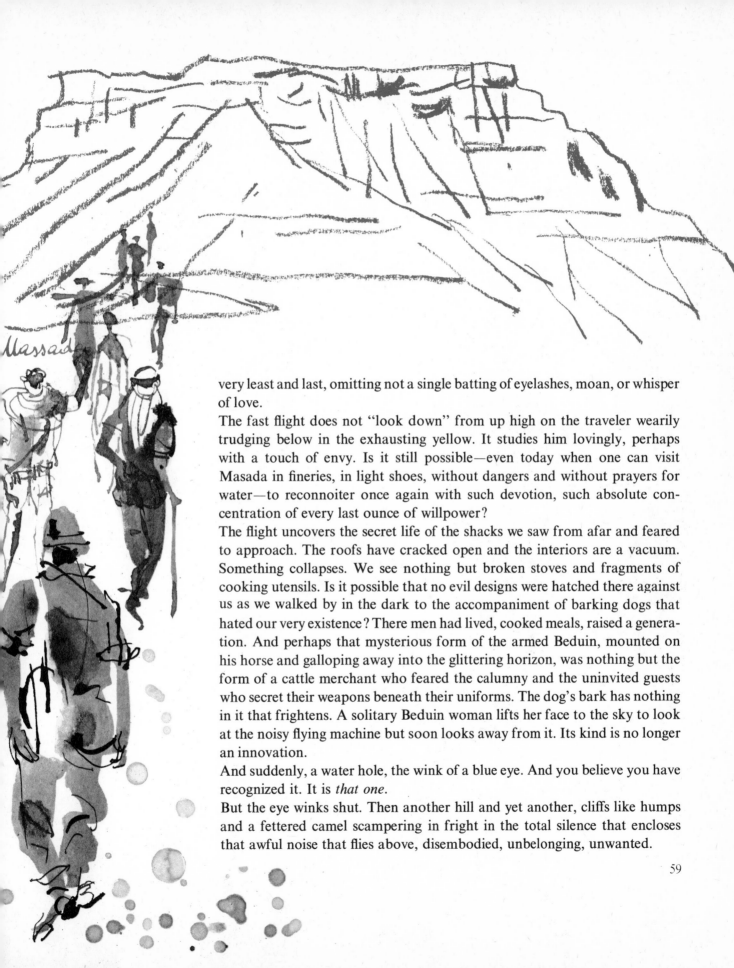

Massada

very least and last, omitting not a single batting of eyelashes, moan, or whisper of love.

The fast flight does not "look down" from up high on the traveler wearily trudging below in the exhausting yellow. It studies him lovingly, perhaps with a touch of envy. Is it still possible—even today when one can visit Masada in fineries, in light shoes, without dangers and without prayers for water—to reconnoiter once again with such devotion, such absolute concentration of every last ounce of willpower?

The flight uncovers the secret life of the shacks we saw from afar and feared to approach. The roofs have cracked open and the interiors are a vacuum. Something collapses. We see nothing but broken stoves and fragments of cooking utensils. Is it possible that no evil designs were hatched there against us as we walked by in the dark to the accompaniment of barking dogs that hated our very existence? There men had lived, cooked meals, raised a generation. And perhaps that mysterious form of the armed Beduin, mounted on his horse and galloping away into the glittering horizon, was nothing but the form of a cattle merchant who feared the calumny and the uninvited guests who secret their weapons beneath their uniforms. The dog's bark has nothing in it that frightens. A solitary Beduin woman lifts her face to the sky to look at the noisy flying machine but soon looks away from it. Its kind is no longer an innovation.

And suddenly, a water hole, the wink of a blue eye. And you believe you have recognized it. It is *that one*.

But the eye winks shut. Then another hill and yet another, cliffs like humps and a fettered camel scampering in fright in the total silence that encloses that awful noise that flies above, disembodied, unbelonging, unwanted.

59

Massada
excavations 1964
עליזה אורבך
גבעות 1964

Massada
excavations 1964

אלקבי
64

Although it is gone and past, the mind returns to the water hole. And perhaps it is indeed *the one*. The source. And you remember that meeting. In the terrible thirst, in the dry. The sticky crust in the mouth, the gurgle in the throat, and the exhaustion. Almost you wished you were dead, but, of course, not. It was simply an heroic expression of a childish desire to lie down, sleep, and wake up miraculously in some other place, near the promised water hole. From that moment when you had lost faith in the guide, who had said with a smile, "There it is, beyond the hill. I know this desert like the palm of my hand," and it *wasn't* there, you became afraid that it was all vain promises, there was no water, nothing. (Later you yourself were the guide, but then you knew better. If you said anything at all, you said, "There are several water holes hereabouts, also cisterns, but sometimes they dry up already by early spring . . .")

A colt, his head lowered, found the water hole. The Beduin, with his long sword, wasn't long in coming. But we were already there, near the rim, in perfect order, so as not to shame the Palmach in the eyes of the Beduin and the colt. That minute in which the taste of rancid water comes into your mouth, your whole being is one single hallelujah to it. You believe that from now on you shall desire nothing nobler than cool clear water. If you shall be permitied but a little water on your burning head and some to paddle your sore feet in, you shall be content with that and a peck of carols. For that divine delight you shall trade all the kingdoms of earth. For never in your life have you known stronger emotions: gratitude, a conciliation with life, the joy in nature that is capable of giving you of its fullness in such abundance—though the hole holds no more than three or four cubic meters. But a drowning man doesn't require a luxury liner—a board will suffice.

And in a few minutes, in the window, Masada, pedestrian, too near, teaming with people. But for an instant as the helicopter dips preparatory to landing, south of the barrage you spy a solitary broom plant. Is it really the one? And you feel that what made up your youth is here, in that piece of land that had known your young body, the stone in your back, the darkling crags rising above you. Rising manhood. First love. Man is no more than the soil of a little country.

A quick look at the diggings: The Byzantine church, the water hole, the baths, Herod's palace, signs (No Entry) and barbed-wire fences. In a minute the parade begins. Familiar notes. Trumpets. The swearing-in-ceremony. The speech of the senior officer who is trying to link the parade to the tradition of the marches of the youth movements and the Palmach. But here they have electricity by the flaming torches. And the activity by the fire is apparently not what it used to be. They have here a wailing saxophone and an entertainment program. What they broadcast in Ramallah, Ankara, the Voice

of America, Damascus, and Kol Israel—the saxophone wailed on the top of Masada.

A rain that whipped us suddenly, out of season, brought the nocturnal Masadian entertainment program to an end. Flurries of wind scourged us with intermittent salvos of mud and water. Jokers among the company said that, no matter what, one cannot come to Masada in a suit and light shoes. If it isn't fire, it's water. One cannot come out unscathed, so as not to lessen the image of that rock citadel that had become a symbol.

At night, the way back is even shorter. Ordinary tranquillity approaches fast, lighted with the wondrous light that pours out through the windows. You cannot see buildings from above, but rather ejections of light, the opposite of the shade that they throw during daytime. From high above, they look like islands of familial tranquillity connected to one another by the fireflies —cars that travel hither and thither like some public business that produces incandescent honey in the enormous comb of settlements.

Touchdown takes us back to the here and now. The landscape wakes up the dark inside the car that drives us to our homes. The flight into the recent and the ancient past is over. We feel like some archaeological mission returning home after making an important discovery.

64

HISTORY.

South of Plugot junction by the winding road there's a eucalyptus wood
marking what once was the center of the Arab village Faluja. Everyone
knows that on blood-sodden battlefields green grass grows and is munched
by cattle. The sudden pangs are in our heart, and likewise, the awe before
the historical. Unless you raise from your own memories a specter to bear
witness, the blood won't call out from the land. Years ago, when I got there
for the first time and walked about that hill—treading very, very softly, for
there were yet no signs that all the mines had been dug up—to watch from
it the hills to the north, I wondered about the feelings of a man watching
earth from space. Spaceships were then yet a dream that the uninitiated were
unaware how near was its fulfillment. To just such an extent, that hill had
been beyond our reach. I could not forget the look of the men, defeated, returning at a run over the plain, carrying the wounded on their shoulders, the
burning vehicles behind them and tufts of black smoke and dust rising before
their faces.

The dead were laid in rows in the wadi. Such vehicles as could move rushed
with the wounded along the watercourse. A broken arm that was hanging,
banging over the side of a half-track, appeared to grow longer and longer.
Two officers sat facing each other silently, listening to heart-wrenching cries
from the wireless receiver. One officer who thought someone had interpreted
an order incorrectly said then something from which the word "historic"
stuck out as something out of place, as some exaggeration, slightly distasteful, in that it does not become men of action. He was right, though, of course.
That campaign swayed matters that were far beyond the piece of land con-
cerned. Nevertheless, we were so accustomed to that declamatory style of
talk that the dictates of good taste demanded we avoid it, especially here,
where time stopped its march, by the rows of the dead.

Matter "historic" was our daily bread. We often participated in some quiet celebration of firstness. We studied at the "First Hebrew Gymnasium," joined the first commando companies in the underground, saw several laying of cornerstone ceremonies of several virgin projects in the Land of Israel; and during the war we never doubted that we were in the locus of an occurrence of some great historic significance. Sometimes it slips by very quietly, though, without our notice. In Kibbutz Gat, in a room that held nothing except a table and some chairs, an historic meeting was held between the staff of the Southern Front Command and the staff of the Egyptian division that was besieged in the Falwja Pocket.

They were older by several years. Their senior officers were older than our senior officers and their junior officers were older than our junior officers. And it seemed as if defeat had given them a still more elderly expression. A supposedly formal talk was conducted in broken English between the commanders, the rest acting as an audience; and several private talks got going between neighbors, cumbersomely, before the negotiations began. We sat mixed together. If I am not mistaken, no one had planned it. We came in together, and since the senior officers had to sit together, we never got to sit in two orderly, opposing groups. My "enemy" talked, in better English than the others but with the peculiar accent of his people, of the condition of the casualties in the Falwja Pocket and of the shortage of medicine. From time to time he exchanged smiles with his neighbor to the left, the adjutant of the Israeli Front Commander, his opposite number in the early negotiations that were held in preparation for the present meeting. I didn't think he believed that he was conducting a "diplomatic" conversation that might bear on the Israeli Command's decision to demand unconditional surrender. However, since good manners made talking obligatory, there was nothing better to talk about than some human interest topic . . . men sick, wounded, miserable. His face was pleasant, trustworthy, and free of hostility, and I somehow got the impression that he was trying to hint that all were ready to surrender but that the final decision rested with the commander. An army is an army.

I didn't need his hints to know whose was the final decision. For without the young officer's recommendation, too, my attention was riveted on that man who sat with the Front Commander and spoke in broken English. I knew that there, behind that table, they were making history and I was sorry

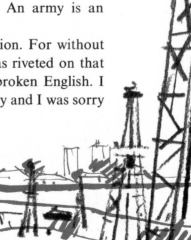

Keletz fields
(Faluja)

about the part of that talk that I was missing because of the social chat of my neighbor, and only manners prevented me from asking him with all due respect to shut up and let me hear what I was missing. I don't remember what was said during that chance conversation, so deeply was I engrossed in the other one. Probably I sounded the usual irrelevancies, the diplomatic platitudes, like "that's the way things are," or "it wasn't us who began this war," or "war is war"; but the distress on my face, caused by the very conversation I had no wish to be involved in and which aligned me with the wounders, the ruthless, who prevent medical supplies, might have appeared to the Arab as a sincere worry over the condition of the wounded regarding whose fate he was keening his dirge.

All that while I was studying the black man, the commandant. Only in his face did I observe real distress. His English, which was poor, made deeper still the expression of sorrow on his countenance. He was coal black, completely Negro, a Sudanese. But he did not have the flattened nose of the Hammitic. Years later, I saw in Ethiopia similar features, in Semitic tribes that live near the sources of the Nile, tall, handsome, and with a wondrously sad expression. His face showed that he well felt the burden of responsibility that weighed on his shoulders: He was the commander. He alone was culpable. If he should hear the cries of the wounded, bow to the inevitable, stop the bloodshed that no longer held either promise or hope—the other officers, the Egyptians, the *whites*, could wash their hands of the whole affair. It would not be they who had taken the decision to surrender.

"It is not a question of equipment," he said, when asked why he could not agree to the evacuation of the Pocket without the military materiel; "it is a question of honor." He said "honor" in such a ludicrous accent that the "h" sounded like a guttural "o." And it was not merely the accent that was ludicrous, but the very manner of talking in such fashion to an enemy. It was the "honor" of opéra bouffe, an amateur theatricalism in dubious taste, outmoded, distasteful. That talk emanated from this wonderful human countenance like some cheap recitation, and the disappointment it brought me caused real sorrow, for in his beautiful, black, sad, and so grave countenance there was a promise of a much higher degree of "humanity." I wondered whether he did not feel the contradiction between the adult, agonized tragic substance of his negro character—this Othello—and that cheap adaptation of a "white" fashion that had already yellowed with age. "Honor" . . . a few cannons and some vehicles against the lives of several hundred men . . .

The historic meeting was over. The commander refused to evacuate his army without its equipment. That night the King made him a brigadier. The guns begun to rumble once again.

When the time came for parting, I nearly forgot to part from my neighbor to the table. The adjutant was deep in talk with him. I continued to follow the black commander with my eyes, I wanted to know what expression has a man because of whose "onor" so many men must die. When we left, I saw my neighbor once more. I remembered he had told me his name but I had already forgotten it. To enable me to keep my stories to my friends as exact as possible, I asked my friend for the name of the Egyptian officer who had sat with us.

"What do you need his name for?" he said. "He isn't one of the important ones. Anyway, you'll forget if you don't write it down. But if you insist: Gamal Abdel Nasser."

I didn't write it down, and I did forget.

HEBRON MOUNTAIN AND GUSH ETZION.

One night in 1942, at the end of a forced company march, we got to a rocky cliff in the Hebron Mountain; a place, we were told, called Hirbat a Habila. We were told, too, that shortly some Jewish settlements were to go up there. Darkness covered the face of the land and all I could see was the stone hedge behind which I lay, my frozen fingers glued to an icy pistol—a lookout for the company against a night attack by the men of Mount Hebron. We had it as tradition that any Jewish penetration of their territories was taken by them as an insult. I lay there for a long while and thought of the feeling of security we derive from having company.

A last fire died out by the wall of an abandoned stone building. The singing had died out long ago. In another minute complete silence descended and all I heard was the sound of a suspicious wind among the oak leaves and some other vague night sounds: an anguished cricket call, left unanswered, a distant moan, and it seemed almost possible to hear the dew descend on the rocks.

We had only a few pistols, but nevertheless we saw ourselves as conquerors of the mountain. Only thirteen years had passed since the massacre of the Jews of Hebron. In those days I was a boy and knew nothing, but I felt that new restrictions had tightened around us. My parents walked about with mournful faces and a relative hid a parcel I was forbidden to look at under the innocent tin bathtub in our apartment. There were photos in black borders in the papers. But thirteen years is not a long time, and what is sealed in the collective memory falls also to the lot of the individual who did not

אלצרי תוגרה בחברון
Hebron

Hebron, in the Cave of Machpela

Gush Etzion
(Mount Hebron)

participate in the event. It was obvious that many men who we had passed on this march to Mount Hebron had held in their cunning looks a dark secret that our minds could not grasp.

We knew they were armed, hostile, lawless, and spoiling for a fight; nevertheless, we felt tremendously secure in our company. Reason shows that our confidence had nothing to rely on, had matters come to an open brawl. But reason decrees, too, that a feeling of security, even if unfounded, does repel a secret enemy.

That same thought came to me in 1948 when I flew with an old friend over the besieged Gush Etzion. We were supposed to drop the besieged some letters, one formal note, and spare parts for the wireless. The Arab legion already lined the Jerusalem-Hebron road and a multitude of villagers had gathered on the hills. They greeted us with such boyish cheer when we flew in that light, awfully vulnerable plane, low over their heads! On the very eve of a catastrophe they skipped, heads held high, arms stretched sideways, like children at a party . . . as if that light plane could bring them salvation.

חברון
Hebron

Cave of Machpela – Hebron

I thought about it: It must be that we represented a symbol of that feeling of security they get from the bigger company, even if but for a moment. The experts knew that all hope was gone. Indeed, many of those who skipped there like playful children we were not to meet again. Others we met a few months later—again in joy, for they had been released from bondage—but reserved and deliberate, they belonging to a minority that had experienced defeat on their flesh.

In the defense of Gush Etzion 236 fell, some in battle and some ruthlessly butchered. Our losses in the conquest of Mount Hebron in 1967 were less than a dozen. An ancient Greek philosopher said that a man's character is his fate; how much more so, his country. The nature of the terrain is such that we are condemned to attack when we would defend ourselves. On the day of the conquest, I was impelled by a bothersome sentiment to see Hebron

73

defeated. That Hebron in which we had to tread softly, and to remove ourselves from as quickly as possible, murderous Hebron that sought our blood, that rioted as a demonstration against the tendency to compromise of their little king who had tried to hold each rope by both ends.

How unpretentious and festive Hebron was when receiving the conquering army! The town was crowned with white flags, abundant with geraniums, its markets empty. The army camped outside the town. Two soldiers in an open jeep, submachine guns hanging negligently from their shoulders, held in terror the streets of the town that for fifty years had been known for its professional brassiness. A man of property fearful for his wealth was serving coffee to officers and to any who might be on a first-name basis with authority. Young blades with enormous mustaches would walk gently, with lowered eyelashes, waving a white handkerchief, dancing, as it were, a dainty dance with a bride named defeat.

The notorious, infamous Hebron was surrendered without revolt, without deep hate, in a cool, mercantile calculation.

And it wasn't many days before infants pestered every passer-by offering merchandise he had no need of at a price which tempted the weak-minded.

רפאל
בחברון הערבית
Hebron

The shops were wide open. The astute merchants, in traders' English—rough and unpolished like Hebron's glass, a tongue in which these men did not know a single, solitary unnecessary word, a word which did not serve direct material usage—were offering the inhabitants of Jerusalem, Nazareth, and Tiberias "souvenirs from the Holy Land."

In a little while the Cave of Machpela was opened and the square at its foot teemed with traders, licensed and amateur both. The holy place imparted its blessing of plenty to all and sundry. Even the most obtuse skeptics had to confess the power possessed by the graves of the patriarchs to bestow material advantage on their courtyard's keepers. And we had been robbed of that degree of noble-mindedness that the world appears to demand of us.

Even had we desired to hide our pride of conquest and to exact from our hearts all that is human and deep in it and sympathetic to the plight of the defeated, we could not have done it, for we were compelled to make our way by force through a crowd of traders that stood, a fortified bastion, in our way to Mearat Hamachpela.

At the door of a souvenir shop stood that type who is stateless and country-less, whose clothes and mustache are well cared for, and whose expression, compounded of a smile that dances behind his glasses, loans his face the appearance of reverence and utter dependability. When was it that we saw him last? Was it in Acco, Athens, Istanbul, Alexandria? Or perhaps Marseille or Naples? Or Massawa or Venice? He looked us over and knew immediately the extent to which we cared to look over either his life story or merchandise. He bestowed upon us a wise smile that contained at once pride of his perspicacity and irony of his pride.

"Do you know the role folklore reserves for this string of glass beads?" he asked, then replied, "It guards you from evil."

"From doing evil, from the evil eye, or from evil that others would inflict upon you?"

He replied, "Evil! You never know whence it comes." And a narrow tongue of fire suddenly lit in his keen eyes.

אשר בעכפלה - חברון
Cave of Machpela
Hebrow

רבקה אמנו

TEL AVIV-JAFFA.

THE HEART OF TEL AVIV.

"The heart of Tel Aviv" is not a sentimental reference to a town's soul. It is a name of an area in the south of the town that in my childhood was the town's center. And since there were already a commercial center and a craftsmen's center, there was no option but to call the new center by that soulful name.

Those who had known the town when younger, prettier, exciting, dancing in the streets, merrymaking on an empty stomach, sang its praises. The little, old, childish, beginning all from the start, in love with itself, sand-swept, sun-drenched, bright in whitewashed plaster—Tel Aviv, the first Jewish town. I remember it, too, when it was somewhat older, a trifle deliberate, avid to grow more and more. It seemed that on every Shabat walk one found a vineyard gone and a new building in its place.

In the town where you were born, though it may grow and spread, something small remains. The growth cannot catch up with the rate of dwarfing that the man's eye commits on the wondrous palaces and gigantic trees of childhood. I remember "ship house" and "the falling house"—the border of the independent scouting range of kindergarten days—that were considered as marvelously palatial; with what a degree of wonder at himself did the child look at them upon return from a trip to Jerusalem. Everything flattened out before his eyes. The biased lattice rim—luxuriant in the architecture of those days—suddenly had become a mere lump of concrete, possessed of no ancient splendor, lacking stones from the hill, lacking the whispering tale-telling of biblical tales.

In Tel Aviv everything was sane, traditionally modern, coated with fresh paint, scrubbed, hygienic. Mysteries we were compelled to invent. Two maniacs who strolled about the town with a mad woman and a fellow in the Jewish Regiment uniform who walked with a walking stick—they alone provided us with a peephole into the dark and mysterious, a world subject to fate's decrees. A garden encircled with a wall, with tall trees sticking out above, called to liberty childish imaginings. It was Europe, the landscape of our parents' childhood. In winter we pictured it to ourselves as smothered in snow.

All the rest, it seemed, was engineered, planned, designed, like the national holidays, like the planting spectacle of Tu Bishvat; like the Adloyada, the quiet demonstrations, the gymnasiums' balls, the unpretentious Bohemians who drank tea at Razki's bar.

Jaffa and Sarona were two separate worlds, as if a steel wall had cut them off one from the other. In the heart of Tel Aviv we felt completely secure, as if we were living on an island protected by a defensive rampart—the bright whiteness of the buildings; the welcome of house fronts, the always-open windows an expression of the fraternal sentiments of the encircled population. Inside the white streets all were friends, everyone cared for his neighbor, for one fate was shared by all. On either side, Jaffa and Sarona, there were stones and dogs. And even when houses burned in the suburbs and young men with somber expressions walked fast in the streets with hoe handles hid in their clothing and far-off sounds of explosion tore through the Shabat tranquillity, we felt completely secure watching laundry dancing in the wind on balconies and roofs. The voice of the old-clothes dealer, sawing the air on the very day in which the papers told with giant headlines of massacres, strengthened in us the secure notion that on our island life went on as usual. Tel Aviv must rid itself of old things, for it must always renew itself.

The smell of Tel Aviv was the smell of fresh lime and also of salty sand and citrus peel. In our cellar, where water intruded in winter, there formed some rancid moss. It was therefore immediately honored to encompass the best of translated literature: The Count of Monte Cristo languished there beside Hirsh Lakert, Jean Valjan, Cinderella, and D'Amitzis's poor. Only the rich and the happy, the likes of Oscar Wilde's princes, Ingeborg, and Richard Coeur de Lion lived in Rothschild Boulevard on the third floor, above the ficuses, facing the eucalyptuses' tops.

Today "the heart of Tel Aviv" is a district of old, gray houses, peeling plaster, its few yards and gardens now paved, serving as parking lots. There is no sense in renovating or whitewashing the buildings, for they are to be pulled down anyway. To their owners they represent an established claim over a building lot on which a fantastic and increasing rate of increased value tax is due. So, in the meantime, everything seems derelict and children no longer play in the streets where cars park in rows, each by its meter. The

ground floors have been leased for business premises, a lawyer has his offices upstairs, and the last of the old tenants, on the third floor, are scraping and pinching pennies to have enough money for a down payment on an apartment in the north. Had they not needed to wait for compensation moneys that owners will have to pay when the lot is cleared, preparatory to the erection there of a skyscraper, they would have left long ago, if only for the sake of their children who now risk their health playing on the tarred roofs and mess up the laundry. Only the barber shop still stands, with the old sign that tells you that here, and here only, is "the heart of Tel Aviv." The old barber, his hands no longer steady, now shaves a balding man who as a child loved to listen to the tinkle of the scissors when the barber prepared to attack his thick locks of hair.

At the back of the "heart," new buildings are already standing. Each is a memorial to some old playing ground. But the old wooden bench in Rothschild Boulevard is still there. A second love does not expropriate the rights of the first one. Sand is now absent even from the boulevard, which has been paved to add to the comfort of strollers. Only at the foot of the trees are left tiny reminders of soil, too little to live on, too much to die for lack of. But man is not merely the soil of a little country. He is also a paving stone of concrete. A small boy who once crossed Karl Neter Street in three bounds, even if he is now sick of the city and has moved out to the country, to a different manner of living, to a window that opens on hill and valley and wood, even he will probably return to cross that street first with two bounds, then with six wary steps. At any rate, when I went there a while ago to see for myself, I saw a little boy trying to cross the street in three bounds in spite of the cars.

Herzlia Gymnasium 1960

Herzl Street
and Shalom Tower/1965

Even when we crossed the waves and swam "very very far," our field of vision stayed blocked in the south by that long finger which Jaffa jabs into the sea. Its silhouette on the skyline—the well-known engraving on a "rare" stamp—with the lighthouse and the mosque at the righthand corner, were a summer vista, a backdrop to the salty adventure of release from scholarly burdens, from responsibility, from the white, shaming hue of our thin extremities that were soon joyfully acquiring lobster coloring in the burning sun. The wild reinless scramble with raised knees and goat bleats into the white, sweeping froth was always observed from there, or so we used to think, with a cold, hostile eye. When we threw off our clothes, deaf to mothers' entreaties ("Beware, you never know from where danger springs; swim only near the lifeguard"), we were yet never quite free of the notion that some places were for us out of bounds. Even the sprinting field was blocked, in the south, by an invisible fence. Beyond a bare rocky stretch of beach, far in the distance, lay a foreign paradise in which we could not set a foot. It served to remind us—especially in those hours when we would throw off us all that was not of our flesh, ready for the sensual delights of immersion in the salty, turbulent, sweeping, infinite—that Tel Aviv was not an island, and that the white wall in whose shade we hid was not a bastion for a happy childhood free of all fear.

In distant childhood lies a memory of a journey to Jaffa port to greet a father returned from Europe. In the shaded carriage I tried both to watch all that strange foreignness flowing in the streets and to hide myself so I wouldn't be noticed. The echoing tak-tak of the horse's hoofs on the concrete road was the forced march of time into the unknown. That royal tail, the horse's buttocks rippling in the air, the hot vapor of greenish yellow that drifted gracefully under the carriage, with the sash of the huge-bellied coachman, were chapters A and B of a tale which, albeit fraught with dangers, was also assured of a happy end.

Tel-Aviv was a town of open windows and bright shining panes. Jaffa was a town of closed green shutters. The nearer you got to Jaffa, the greater the width of the bar across the doors of shops whose owners admitted customers through a side entrance: a locked gate and a narrow suspicious wicket by its sides. These were Jaffa memories until your first meeting with the market. Here one could dispense with wariness. The colorful backdrop was joyful. The smell ordered a feast. The clashing cymbals of tamarhindi sellers accompanied their musical racket with a capricious rhythm. Even the backbent thumb of the drink-seller, with an overgrown black nail, wiping the lees from the cup before he'd tilt the rattling brass jar forward to fill the cup with the cool, reddish-brown liquid, looked friendly. And the carpet-seller, shaking

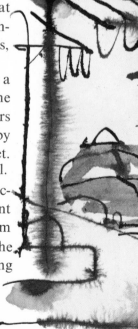

Persian dust straight in his patroness's face, keeping up a monotonous hymn of praise in a tongue unknown in this world, was regarded as some tremulous reception in the inner chamber of that childish legend in which the gate-keepers are forever evil and out to trick you. Inside the palace there is always a gay, laughing princess. All that is needed is to scamper in, somehow, between the legs of the murderous giant.

The cups were the very brass utensils, dusty green, decorated with stylized letters and elusive configurations, from which the wondrous figures from *The Thousand and One Nights* drunk "love in delight"—a magic potion not quite meaningful to a child, which the storyteller let both his heroes drink, the dark-eyed lover and the doe-eyed loving, before he laid them to sleep at the end of each story. And behind every dark vault, inside the concavity to wash one's hands in, by the concrete water tap lay in wait the doorway to the child's treasure of precious stones and pearls, there for the taking of whosoever is not dark and evil.

The essence of commercialism. Horror replaced by the laughing countenance of temptation. With a wink and a gesture a light-haired woman is invited to have her fortune read by a decayed, pockmarked, scabies-blighted old bag; and the very sight of the folds of skin on her body, like worn-out rags, and her osseous arms disfigured with tattoo marks cracked and indecipherable with age, are enough to drive from a young woman's heart and mind any desire to peep into the future. Women in bare feet and black veils walked proudly before lustful eyes. Stall owners were preparing reddish-gray shashlik

יפו – כיכר
השעון =

Jafo-Clock Square

on coal pans in the middle of the street, licking dirty fingers to rouse the appetites of passers-by. In the coffeehouses, on woven stools by beaten brass tables, sat effendis capped in red tarbooshes with black tufts, their stomachs resting comfortably on thighs and knees, inhaling the intoxicating fragrance of the nargiles planted by their feet and the road dust raised by a solitary passing car (the District Governor's?) that frightened with its noise a cackle of chickens hanging lively and indignant by their legs from a butcher's door jamb.

The effendis' nimble fingers have already counted the amber prayer beads an infinite number of times, as if counting the wealth that fell to them, ridding them of the need to indulge in the wheeling-dealing that ebbed and renewed itself with tremendous gusts of noise all over the place in a mad ignoble scramble after material possessions.

Here the Tel Aviv Jews were always welcome, being potential customers. And the real oriental bazaar that was carried on in Jaffa every day of the year was not at all similar to its namesake in the north of Tel Aviv. There stood buildings of thin walls, the wind nearly blowing off their tin roofs; and in a single day, following the termination of that "oriental bazaar," it was like a desolate ghost town, strewn with paper, rags, empty bottles, and yellowing posters, like a stadium after the tournaments are over. In Jaffa it was the real thing, not an exercise nor a spectacle nor a fair, but real life with the sharp, hot olives and all the forbidden things.

The olives, a hundred kinds of olives, like the salty cheeses, the leben, the reddish turnips, the fustuk chalabi, the woolly red sugar threads woven into a mop around a wooden splinter—all these were forbidden. They teemed with "germs." Tomatoes from Jaffa market were doomed to a soap bath, fruit were subjected to chemical disinfection. The sheets of dried apricot, the leader, likewise the sos sticks were in the nature of a lethal poison, and by decree they were to remain forever a spectacle that can't be fathomed, that might be seen but must not be used. And forever they and their smell became the symbols of a closed city, whose shutters were drawn, where hate-filled eyes peeped from within, through the lattice. During the 1921 riots, when the first bodies were brought to the yard of the municipal hospital and the wounded were carried on stretchers along the streets, immediately the smell of the blood mingled with the fragrance of the tamarhindi, the reek of the shashlik and the taste of the intoxicating anise.

The smell of the fish and the kebab, the sight of the crabs, the octopi, the flatfish, the clocktower, and a prisoner in chains became as one with the whistle of the ship that set out into the mysterious double blue, after its massive-armed sailors threw down upon Jaffa's beaches its cargo—light-skinned pioneers in gray peaked caps who looked in adoration at the Jewish boy whose luck so favored him as to have him born in Eretz Israel.

In the Old City

JAFFA'S ALLEYS.

The Jaffa of today is a town that supports its own citizenry and amuses the dwellers of Tel Aviv. These same alleys in which a Tel Avivite used to fear to set foot, today he parks his car in—still with great care, lest it get scraped by a passing vehicle—when he goes to one of the places of entertainment that have entrenched themselves near the gates of the port. Even the exotic sight of the ancient buildings that have not been destroyed during the War of Independence and have not toppled down with age amount to entertainment for one whose eye had its fill of the modern city that improvises in a single style upon square blocks whitewashed with a few light hues. Those who are not oversensitive can be entertained here, too, by the stylized manner of the place's poverty: Rags that possess a personal expression, laundry stretched hanging from wall to wall, the colorfulness of grime, the secrecy that emanates from the lives of persons who, uprooted from some far existence, have never troubled to build themselves a new home. In chill dark houses walk the ghosts of tenants who skedaddled in the middle of the night. On the lavatory walls you can still read filthy epithets in Arabic. And every once in a while, when the new tenant adds a little soil to a flower pot—perhaps to remind himself of childhood's landscapes, on the edge of the green and the forest by a tranquil wide-flowing river—he meets with some

89

crumb of the estate of the previous landlord: an old coin, a rusted key, the mouthpiece of a waterpipe, a rifle cartridge.

You can find here, too, the fringe existences. The half- or double-life of the drug addicts. Here they are permitted to indulge, within limits, in self-destruction, providing they do not inflict themselves upon others. The police are interested mostly in the dealers in white illusions. The insensible, drunk or otherwise under the influence, lying here in the gutter in nauseatingly peaceful slumber, dreaming their ethereal visions, are a subject for the cameras of the souvenir hunters, who seek here something dark, primordial, mysterious, like the ancient stench that belches out of the drains that had carried clear water for the Romans but served the Turks as a sewer. If you added a pinch of theatrical moral indignation and shook a fist at the heavens, you could envision the whole spectacle on an avant-garde stage in Tel Aviv.

In the adjacent nightclubs the atmosphere is typically Mediterranean. A cosmopolitan program, featuring the oldest subject there is, from a position equal to any and all in five or six basic languages familiar to all who pay their radio tax. A Greek torch singer undresses in French, while singing a Serb folksong; lethal jealousy reflects from the Bulgarian pianist's eyes— the male clients who latch the totally impersonal lecherous stare that the place makes obligatory onto the double revelation afforded by the cleavage of her dress. A young Israeli who has visited Paris twice already and is now showing the sights, on behalf of the Foreign Ministry, to an African diplomat in whose country women still walk bare-breasted even in the main street of the capital, is pleased that the guest is not bored. A young state, but already there is something to see at night, in Jaffa.

In more refined clubs men who had gone here the whole way—pioneering, Hagana, illegal immigration, war, underground—find pleasure in the fact that they can sit on a woven stool and joke about the innocence that had induced them to come there. In the flea market it is still possible to buy, at a price commensurate with their degree of decay, brass utensils that have had a touch of green slapped on them after being purchased for a pittance from their Arab owners, who had previously scraped and polished them with the best detergents and polish materials available so that they could be rid of them and buy in their place modern plastic utensils. Bulgarian carpets are sold to immigrants from Persia who make their living selling Persian carpets. An old Italian piano, the wires, keys, and all else that might cause redundant noise long removed from it, is placed here on sale at an absurdly low price, to complete a Baroque-style set of furniture that stands here half inside and half outside the seedy shop that sells horseshoes for luck as well. Venetian glass, crystals from Prague, some of them in modern plastic designs, aid impoverished aristocrats to build up again the commercial empire destroyed by

Nazi Germany. And an ex-tenor of Hungarian extraction loudly proclaims his newly acquired Sephardic name, adopted in the hope that it will lend credence to the original taste of the kebab his wife prepares guided by a recipe she has received from her recently-arrived-from-Iraq neighbor. A town of foregathered diasporas. A chance meeting of a dozen cultures that fight a battle to the death in this non-Jewish street over their rights of origin and degrees of descent. A town in which the joy aroused in the street by an encounter of two childhood friends calls for recollections of another town, a town in which a joke in Yiddish is an insult in Arabic; and eastern style hanky-panky, the cheating of the professed expert, is thought by Rumanians stealing. A town that has no common joys nor common memories.

In the main street not far from where, standing in the Palmach headquarters, we watched in wonder the daily infiltration of new citizens into an abandoned town, a public entertainment stage was built at Purim. Entertainers, who drove in fast cars from stage to stage, having already collected ovations in the plush north of Tel Aviv and in the central suburbs, faced here an audience of a dozen tongues and managed at best to extract a few polite smiles. Careworn faces of working mothers eagerly looked forward to the fancy-dress competition. Silently, in their hearts, they again calculated the cost of materials, the amount of work invested, and the size of the prize. The child facing the limelight, subjected to the vapid patter of a professional entertainer who laughed at the provincialism of the Jaffa inhabitants, apparently wasn't happy in his regal robes either. Perhaps he also remembered the row at home. The father wanted to skimp. The mother wanted to give her son one day of being royalty. Even though she was beaten by her husband, she made the costume, to spite him. After all she was in Israel, where an oriental woman is free to get beaten and do as she will.

Not far from there, oblivious of the noise of the street, a family was modestly celebrating its festival. Through the windows a Purim shpiel could be observed—children and adults together, in the manner once common in another town and probably in another language. The deference shown by the father as he placed his little crowned daughter on the table! An uncle stood by and applauded, his hand gently caressing the shoulder of a boy standing by him gulping as fast as he could the "Haman Ears" served around in straw baskets by the lady of the house. The wind blew the curtains back to their place, shutting off the spectacle of familial tranquillity. It isn't nice to peer at windows, anyway. Behind the curtain, however, a new life is stirring.

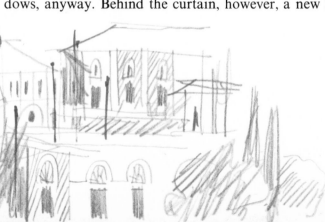

the Israel Museum
Jerusalem

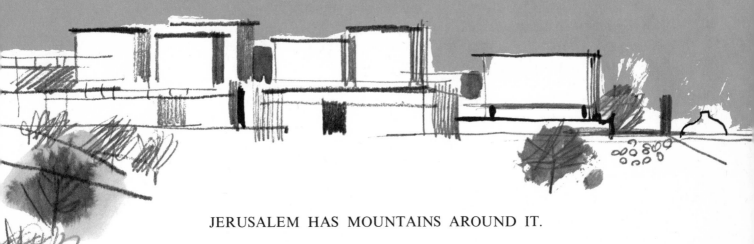

JERUSALEM HAS MOUNTAINS AROUND IT.

BETWEEN FOREST AND DESERT.

When I visited Jerusalem for the first time, my hometown, Tel Aviv, was just twenty-four years old. In the yards of the very oldest houses in Achuzat Beit you could still find big nails that had fallen out of the builders' scaffolding. A tree in Tel Aviv that peered at a third-floor window threw a shade ennobled by venerable age, and a pond covered with green weeds was thought an old, old matter.

But the Jerusalem I suddenly glimpsed from the train window was as ancient as a planet; my eight years of a sudden contracted to a brief, single wonder-exhalation of time. Only the stories of the Bible have popped at one go into the present. In Jerusalem even newly built houses at once acquired an aspect of venerability, for they were built of hewn Jerusalem mountain stone, which comes out of the bowels of the mountain only there to return. Tel Aviv was a town of children in the street, laundry in the yard, the hurried walk of persons rushing on their business. Jerusalem was tranquil, slow, not laughing in the street, as if those priests of a dozen religions and sects, in their long robes, who seek to disavow their position in both place and time, have forced all the people of Jerusalem to be strict with their feelings and to act like they do, restrainedly, discreetly, quietly, with circumspection. In Tel Aviv a man walks the streets, it seems, with his own personal mood. When he comes to Jerusalem it forces upon him a general, historical mood. As if the marks of time there are so numerous that they require constant study. The ancient towers are sphinxes that pose questions to the traveler before he is permitted to set his foot within the walls. Perhaps I have never lived in Jerusalem long enough to lose that feeling that I am immersed in a slow shuffle inside a sealed, high-ceilinged chapel in which the silent swish of my stealthy steps returns to me sharply echoing, as some intruding, rowdy noise in the middle of the holy ritual.

93

TO THE WALL.

In Jerusalem, too, the commonplace existed: By the very gates of the Old City cameos against the evil eye were purchased and philters for a better fortune sold, false merchandise was weighed in crooked scales, and ritual articles were traded at black-market prices in seventy different tongues; taxi drivers cursed as roundly as in Jaffa; the Englishman with a cork hat and uplifted nose stood here, too, belonging yet not belonging, despising both these and the others; and here, too, true Jerusalemites would return from their occupations to their wives and homes, and the tightly wrapped parcels under their arm would be not holy scrolls but stale sandwiches and the leftovers from lunch. But the pilgrim from Tel Aviv would pass all these as if they had never existed. As one who skips from rock to boulder to rock, he would worry his feet from Yad Avshalom through Gat Shamna to Kalba

"מאה שערים"
Meah Shearim
Jerusalem.

95

Jerusalem
Absalom's Pillar and Zachariah's Tomb

Savna's grave and thence to Jaffa Gate and to the Wailing Wall. The market that so enchanted him in Jaffa was here a sort of obstacle that had to be brushed through in the rush, with lowered eyes and palpitating breath on the way to the Wailing Wall.

The Wailing Wall! The stories of childhood, the J.N.F. posters, the picture postcards, the famous paintings, none of these ever hinted how narrow the place, how lacking in imposing splendor, and how pitiful the sight of the poor women who stick slips of paper in the cracks between the great hewn stones! Nor how yellowed the green of the meager shoots that sprout from the Wall . . .

And when the real Wall had lost its splendor, a new dream took root in the childish heart. A purer grandeur, of our own time, earthly, fashioned after the new Jerusalem, self-confident, proud as Jewish Rachavia which, draped in green, will dwell in the secret tranquillity of knowing its own heart and will.

The Wailing Wall

Shiloach

SEEK THE PEACE OF JERUSALEM.

If we shall try merely to note that which the eyes see we shall fill many thick volumes. A legion of historians toiling on its story shall leave their descendants many lifetimes of toil. Every single gate of the Old City locks within itself memories much beyond the capacity of a heavy tome. Each stone in every wall stores stories of ancient times and new. Even a stone lying in a field, it seems, has not lain there because there it first came into being. More probably it had been thrown there when someone was being stoned. Each moment of peace remembers a minute of strife. "Everything flows," whisper the waters in the Shiloach—flows yet returns upon itself again.

We cannot walk it step by step eliciting its stories. There are so many of them that we cannot give them the proper presentation during a journey of new discoveries. All its stories deserve to be heard, for they bear the stamp of the place upon them. We can only, therefore, try and draw, in a handful of lines, a sketch of that Jerusalem which is a mood and a feeling.

Even such as had never seen her called on her as on the symbol of perfection. Poets of a dozen tongues professing a dozen diverse faiths proclaimed her a synonym of spiritual exultation. Even when she was divided, their hearts contained a prayer for the glory of the whole. Even the most secular of

Mosque of Omar

Jerusalem—Lions Gate

nonbelievers, such as go to prayerhouses to admire the artwork and enjoy
the music, treasure Jerusalem as an item of faith. In Jericho you bathe in
its fragrance, the dust of its gold descends in Shomron. The splendor radiating
from the reddish tinge of its stones ennobles even the head of he who comes
to do his trade there.

102

שער ציון
Zion Gate

Dung Gate

When we could approach it only from the west, although its greater part was open and but a minor part removed, we felt we were seeing only its silhouette. For Jerusalem is a city whose full perfection is seen from the mountains surrounding it. And unless you have seen how it gathers unto itself a forest from one side and a desert from the other, you have never seen a town by the spirit put together. It straddles borders; from here a nomad existence, from there a settled civilization. Halfway between the temporary and the life eternal. Whatever lies within it not hallowed by virtue of the faiths of seventy peoples and tongues is sanctified by its power to gather them all in, place them one at the side of the other, and demand of them that they live in a city of peace.

David had built, Solomon fortified, Yehoash smashed, Uziyahu filled up. Nebuchadnezar wrought destruction, Nechemia resuscitated the fire-scorched stones. Shimon the Just maintained, Apolonius broke down. Jonathan built up the walls, the Syrians pulled them down. Herod erected towers, Titus knocked them down with the walls. Adrianus rechristened it Alia Kapitolina, but her turrets were built atop the walls of Jerusalem. The Oumayas built up temples that the Seljouks took by sword and fire. The Crusaders built there a mighty city and Salah-ed-Din tossed its crown to the dust. The Persians, the Mongols, and the Mamelukes came, then were gone, leaving in their wake a trail of destruction. Before it is wholly destroyed it is already rebuilt again. The Ramban found it a pile of rubble "...any that's more sacred than its neighbor being more greviously destroyed..." and Ashtori Haparchi could find no place in it for tranquil studies because it exceeded in crowds and bustle. In 1833 it was plundered by Sudanese, in 1838 its merchants had prospered. Myriads flowed there at the turn of the century only to flee for their lives in 1914. In 1948 it was thought of as torn in two forever, and in one day of summer these swarmed hither and those yonder as a matter of itself understood.

In our childhood it was a symbol of that which had been planted in a distant past. Even its buildings looked as if they had slowly grown out of the stones of the field. Its trees are no fund-raised saplings planted in Tu Bishvat, but the glorious endeavors of stubborn mountainous soil. Its paving stones are the roof of a temple whose splendors lie hidden under earth; even its dirty grime is the struggle of a yesterday to exist for all eternity.

Its inhabitants did not walk the streets on holidays and festivals. A town of mixed population, the holidays of one have no interest for another. Its Sabath days would close within their quarters—for the Sabath of the one was the weekday of the other. A Jerusalem child, it seemed, had eyes more beautiful and sadder than ours. His childhood knew the gravity of those who have foreign life observed through their windows. We had played with sand, he with stone. We used to think our bright, sun-drenched lives the natural

Safed – the "Ari" Synagogue

Safed, the "Ari" Synagogue

Via Dolorosa

order of the universe, while he already knew that his life was that which was obscure to his neighbor. In 1967 we crashed through to it, haunted by visions of imagination. Suddenly we had become personae dramatis in a legend we told our children. We rushed on our way to the Wall, to Mount Scopus, the Mount of Olives, Tur Malka, the Vale of Shiloach, the Valley of Rephaim, to all that had been beyond our reach and was slowly being obscured by the golden mist of forgetfulness and oblivion. And in one miraculous instant all had coalesced into one single entity—we, and that distant time, and Jerusalem. The veils of mist had torn and Jerusalem was the one we had seen, the one we remembered even when we had forgotten. A whole town seeking peace.

Bethlehem—Rachel's Tomb

בית הקברות ירושלים

Jerusalem Church of „Holy Sepulchre"

SCHEM IS NAPLES.

"See Naples, then die," says the proverb; the Naples of Italy, because the excruciating exaltation its beauty works in the beholder is beyond a human's capacity to contain. In the Naples of the Shomron Mountains the chance of death was far more substantial. At least, for a Jew. Not just in days of riots but also in days considered normal; by a knife, a stone, a club. Naples of Shomron was built by Titus west of the ruins of Schem, that Kuttite town which had been distinguished as the eternal rival of Jerusalem and had been destroyed by the Romans. The Arabs bastardized the name to Nablus. It is indeed a town of glorious beauties lying in a bay of mountains. It hasn't been blessed, like its Italian sister, with a volcano to decorate its fringe; but then, instead, it can justly claim to be itself a seething, raging pyre.

Schem has been embarrassed by proverbs. It has been likened to a snake, a serpent writhing along the watercourse between Eibal and Greezim; to the bosom of a woman whose breasts are bare but whose lap is shaded; and to an ambush that closes upon the road from either side. You pass through it, and houses' windows watching you from the side of the road that passes through the valley are like embrasures that have now been condemned to a compulsory cessation of work, enforced by the Israeli steel chariot now ambling sedately in front of you, so maneuvering its gargantuan weight that it shall not harm a child's tricycle.

Schem—a city of refuge that had become a city of insurgence and violence. In our own years it symbolized a hatred deep as death. As if from the distance would emanate its serpentine rage, reeking from the breach opening in the blue wall of the Shomron Mountains. Sedately we journeyed between Netanya and Hadera, so long as its memory had been gone from us. When we remembered it, it was as if a steamy vapor breathed at us from the east. Schem —the focus of eternal malice, an oven of hell astride two fertile hills, whose own beauty detracts not the least from their envy of the Hefer Valley.

A TRAGEDY OF VILLAINS.

If we be permitted to coat with flesh and blood notions created by our own breath, in the manner of our forefathers, we shall be right in saying that history—that shrewd, vain female—had not thought it sufficient to accord Schem that pathos it requires in its great moments. She was tired of it. And as a contemporary, a skeptic, her soul craved a little irony.

It was impossible to conceive in mind a spectacle more ironic than the one that had occurred in Schem: that Schem—that for years had nursed in its bosom a seething hatred; that for forty years had prepared for the day of reckoning; that had taught babies not yet weaned songs of retribution and vengeance; that gnashed its teeth, honed its knives; that boasted of victories in battles not yet fought; that roistered in the alleys and screamed madness

Schem
june 1967

in the streets, and shook its fists toward heaven—that Schem, lusty, tautly prepared to make battle, stood along both sides of the conquering column and received the Israeli soldiers with cheers and ovations.

What a bitter mistake.

They had been seduced to believe that these were men of Iraq's armies,

which were to come to assist at the "freeing of Palestine"—those strange men in unfamiliar uniforms who broke like thunder into Schem's streets, in tanks and armored troop carriers, yet without firing a single shot. It wasn't until an Israeli soldier tried to disarm a smiling policeman whose face, before that, breathed inexpressible joy, that the inhabitants of Schem realized their oh, so bitter error.

It was an error that could not be rectified. By the time they had rushed to their houses and begun sniping, the column had already passed through, turning left to lie in wait for a division of the Arab Legion that was retreating along the highway from Jenin. By and by, other forces began the job of decontaminating the town itself.

112

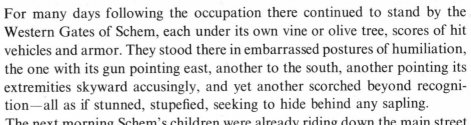

For many days following the occupation there continued to stand by the Western Gates of Schem, each under its own vine or olive tree, scores of hit vehicles and armor. They stood there in embarrassed postures of humiliation, the one with its gun pointing east, another to the south, another pointing its extremities skyward accusingly, and yet another scorched beyond recognition—all as if stunned, stupefied, seeking to hide behind any sapling.

The next morning Schem's children were already riding down the main street on wooden crates mounted on four circular bearings, navigating their precarious way with a string, as if there had never been a war. The faces of the youngest among them, for whom impersonal hate had been nothing but an abstraction, bore an expression that cannot be described by such terminology as is listed in the dictionary of a man of war. It was neither hate nor fear, cunning nor pain, defeat nor a deep-seated promise to avenge the humiliation in a day yet to come. It was something entirely different, born of the astounding behavior of the Israeli soldiers. Down that main street whose traffic died they floated as freeborn. Free of any yoke they took the spellbound town, contemptuous of their parents' terror. A town entered, defeated, had become paradise for the refugees' children who drove their improvised chariots past Zahal's armor which, just one day after the war, was no longer meant to harm.

The refugees went back to their shaded houses, there to cool their hate and obfuscation. Disgrace and shame were concealed in the innermost of rooms. There only remained the abandoned battlefield, and on it the burned metal, the clutter of shredded papers, blood-soaked blankets, abandoned packs, the meager kit-bag of a soldier who no longer had anything further to lose.

Ancient Samarian Script

AN ARAB VILLAGE.

THE SMOKE OF EUCALYPTUSES.

Once I knew them by the dozen: their names on the map, their silhouette on the mountain ridge, the smell of eucalyptus smoke and cattle dung rising from them as some distant warning, the barking of dogs chasing a stranger till he was beyond the flowery path that came from the bosom of the orchards paved with goats' dung. The acacia hedges that enclosed the orchard from which we picked the yellow flowers we made "perfume" from in tiny flasks; the prickly-pear hedges that guarded the fruit gardens, abundance of fruit free of charge but not of punishment; the squills at the edges of their fields and the ancient olive trees inside their vineyards all would greet us when we first set out to learn the countryside. Sometimes the path would lead us inexorably to the very heart of the village. Well we knew that in one minute the dogs would chase us with angry barks and dash within a footstep of our legs, and that in yet another minute we would be right inside the main square, studied from all sides, neither invited nor wanted. Barefoot children in filthy

Arab village
(Jatt)

shirts that reached their navels would chase us a piece; boys would stare at us with animosity, and the elders, looking at us from the doorsteps, the water-pipe between their teeth, would sneer coldly—for our staunchly upright march with heads held high, with steps not too hurried, with eyes straight to the front would not hide from their experienced eye the fear fluttering in our breasts.

These villages had always been veiled with secrecy, like the chill that blew from the old oak-ceilinged, locked and shuttered dark huts, like the smell of za'atar and sos, like the surprise awaiting the eater in the heart of an out-wardly delicious watermelon, like the vague look that annulled our existence as individuals and made us one of a people and nothing more, parts of a dis-liked general whole—such looks as we saw in the eyes of the strange men who spoke a language we did not know and dressed in a manner that to us was foreign. The childish imagination painted anything it couldn't get closely acquainted with in violet colors. The dark was a threatening danger and every rustle bore forth a poisonous viper. On rare occasions one of the natives of such a village would step out of that suspicious anonymity to surprise us with a degree of hospitality we thought to be a heritage of the past or else by a gesture of such nobility that a divided mind did not know how to con-tain it. The good and the evil would stand as direct opposites as in an oriental fable which does not fit with life as it is lived except as a symbol.

One night during a reckless trip in the very center of a purely Arabic terri-tory, the *shabab,* the village blades, decided to practice on us some incidental robbery and even stared intently at the barelegged girls, and the Britisher had long ago climbed into his car and driven to a place of safety. There appeared suddenly at our side, like a character in a fable that perforce must have a happy ending, one of those elders who had previously stared at us with glassy eyes, and he took us to his home to give us shelter. And the next morning, at dawn, he walked with us, the very same glassy look in his eyes, till we were well outside the village.

In time these very villages were the target of our attack. Out of their omi-nous silhouettes, on the skyline of a starry night, shot tiny tongues of fire and incandescent tracks intent on checking our advance. In the following year, many of them had become mounds of rubble, ruins, arid wells, vaults of gates on a background of blue, a multitude of agama on forsaken walls, nests of snakes, desolate orchards, prickly-pear hedges that huge tractors crushed and uprooted. Slowly the walls sank. Where a new settlement had not been established they appeared as remnants of a very distant past that mingled in a landscape of a similar hue, like historic sites that, coated with the dust of the new and alive, are not uncovered again before they have suffi-ciently aged.

In a place that once had witnessed a hand-to-hand fight were now parked

117

tractors and combines, petrol stations, and the tents of Hebrew agricultural farmers working abandoned fields far away from their homes. And it is as if the whole landscape has changed now that the fear that had to be hidden at any cost is no more. The smell of eucalyptus smoke no longer hastens a sudden heartbeat nor readies our senses to prepare to jump over the thorn hedge that life has placed in our way. No more rising manhood and a stand of studied courage against the wild bravery of the sons of nature. Now it is merely the smell of poverty, wretchedness, and the acceptance with enmity in lowered lashes. The mystery has been lit by the pale light of electricity.

ELECTRICITY TO ALL.

The dust has settled down together with the memories of last night. New roads did not reach the threshold of the ruined village on the top of the hill.

Water and wind ground to the quick everything that was fated to annihilation. Angry young men from beyond the border know their birthplace only by hearsay. The almond and walnut trees have withered and been uprooted and citrus has invaded the plots of the olive trees. Not even the wildest of winds will raise a gleaming ember in the place of the great fire. In the Arab villages not abandoned during the war, a new generation has grown. Concrete buildings still dressed in scaffolding stand by the ancient earthen brick huts. The oriental taste is apparent only in the color scheme: the walls of violet and yellow, of azure next to purple. There is electricity, gas, and a refrigerator in the kitchen and a wireless and TV set in the living room.

The coal fire pan and the glowing embers are found now in regular use only in the poorest villages. Elsewhere they are holiday utensils, used on special occasions for the preparation of a feast in the traditional manner. Where once was heard the prayer at its hour, the traditional dirge, and joy was expressed in improvised verses, today all is heard in the shouting radio: prayers and lamentations, music and song. The elders still seek the music of yesterday and the tales of Arabia; the young make do with the trash of popular songs and translated novellas. What is good in Caracas is good also in Taybe.

A person strolling today along the alleys of an Arab village will find that here fathers and sons are divided in their dress and language. Urbanites are not as divided as the villagers, for European clothing and a foreign tongue had reached the town already before the establishment of the State of Israel. In the village it is the events of recent years that have wrought the change.

The fathers, in the traditional dress, are Arabs at home and Arabs when away from home; the sons, dressed after the current fashion, are Arabs at home, but just people elsewhere.

Women no longer use veils. Old women still glance away from a stranger who does not look at them anyway. Yong women fix their hair, though with admirable modesty, and are ready to be photographed by the vine sprigs that cling to the building walls, once they first smear with a mighty palm the face of the younger brother who would try and share with them that dose of unexpected attention.

On the Feast of the Sacrifice it is possible to see at the house of an acquaintance a modern version of an ancient tradition. Even the young and free in manners who still regard Marxist literature as a later revelation take care to observe traditions on this occasion. In the morning they go to prayer and commune with their families at the place of mourning, and afterwards they wander over the family houses, pay visits to daughters married to others, not of the clan, to increase their honor in their husbands' eyes and to hint that they still have protectors: and finally congregate, a multitude, at the house of the head of the clan. The parents maintain the custom by tradition without worrying about its nature or essential substance, while the young are trying to inject a new content into, or at least give their own interpretation to, the molds of an ancient tradition.

Our host was exempt from obligatory courtesy visits, for custom decrees that he who has guests from elsewhere—his relatives should trouble themselves and come to him. Very near the tarmac road, among fruit gardens heavy with fruit sprayed by chemical preparations, in a parlor containing electronic equipment that can put him in touch with the entire world, the Arab villager is still proud of his precepts of hospitality—customs molded in the desert tent, in the heart of the wilderness, a place where the unexpected visit of a guest come to seek protection is a holiday to the soul and a charge on chivalry that a community-of-men-in-becoming cannot do without.

We were seated on pillows, as is customary, in the gallery of a high-walled room, its floor smoothed concrete, its ceiling kermes oak, in the cool, wide-spaced, patriarchal void in which the new furniture crowded by its walls appeared to be something transitory, neither in place nor in keeping. The landlord, our host, toiled in front of us preparing lamb in the traditional manner over a pan of embers.

Even the smoke dispersed and melted in this festive exultation as if it were but a denuded smoke, without the smell of burning, lacking the fragrance of the roast, like a shadow of smoke, a hint only, a symbol of itself, longing for a smoky tradition that has passed away from the world.

Outside, boys and girls strolled about in their very best clothes, and even the tiniest girls were made up and painted. The patriarchs walked with a measured step, the head lowered, hands behind their backs, their fingers shifting and moving the amber prayer beads; as if from eternity to eternity they walked this way, indifferent and festive as men who though preparing for an everlasting life are still versed and knowledgeable in the intricacies of the life ephemeral.

The conversation got around to the historic, economic, and even social origins of the Feast of Sacrifice. Our host filled us with rarefied "Greek" wisdom and there was not even one of the rituals and ceremonies left which was not both dissected and analyzed, made self-explicit to all and sundry, that had not been transfixed by the skewer-sharp eye of a scholar versed and trained in the disciplines of sociology.

We discussed the problems of the Arab village in the State of Israel. The backwardness, the poor education, misplaced "Hebrewism," and the autocratic rule of the patriarchs that stands, an immovable obstacle in the path of ambitious youngsters who would bring the Arab village, in one fabulous leap, into the modern era, lighted by the wondrous glow of the electric bulb.

120

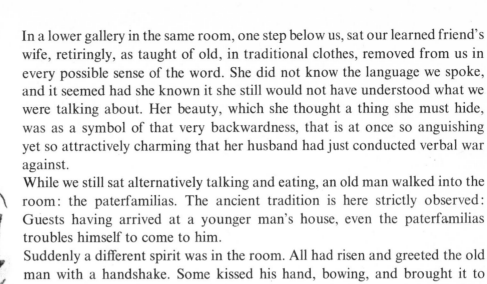

In a lower gallery in the same room, one step below us, sat our learned friend's wife, retiringly, as taught of old, in traditional clothes, removed from us in every possible sense of the word. She did not know the language we spoke, and it seemed had she known it she still would not have understood what we were talking about. Her beauty, which she thought a thing she must hide, was as a symbol of that very backwardness, that is at once so anguishing yet so attractively charming that her husband had just conducted verbal war against.

While we still sat alternatively talking and eating, an old man walked into the room: the paterfamilias. The ancient tradition is here strictly observed: Guests having arrived at a younger man's house, even the paterfamilias troubles himself to come to him.

Suddenly a different spirit was in the room. All had risen and greeted the old man with a handshake. Some kissed his hand, bowing, and brought it to their brow, as custom decrees, with a courtesy majestic beyond description. And the old man passed along, tranquil and festive, the traditional greeting whispering on his lips, then sat by the guests in silent distinction. And although he did not understand our language, nevertheless he would not stir until we got up to leave.

The contention between the generations has not deposed the courtesy of a thousand years. And the young man who preaches of tradition as of an out-

dated sociology is not ashamed to pay age the respect due it in front of guests.

Possibly other young Arabs would have preferred it, could they dare and treat the old in a modern manner. But we, perhaps, would have been well content if, while they had received from us electricity and the bow tie, they would have given us in return that manner of respect towards life, of which the reverence paid to age is such a symbol.

THE TALE OF THE MARKET.

On the first day after the war an atmosphere of threat and violence still persisted, but on the next day a small stall for the sale of cold beverages was stood at the roadside—and thus the market celebrated its victory. For you can't have wheeling-dealing without presenting a cordial countenance to potential customers. And now each passer-by, even if he be in uniform, might be induced to become a customer.

You might say that a trader's smile does not proceed from the heart; but then, so what? Even if it is only stage decor, it yet confers on the street a style of its own. And, doing so, it does more to rid the highway of memories of war than the bulldozers that are piling remains of scorched armor from the wayside. The atmosphere of the market is an atmosphere of seduction. An effort of intention directed to meet the desires of another; the removal of barriers between people; a rapprochement via guessing secret desires; a bid of plenty that breeds a shortage and demand.

The fleeting fraternization that makes buyer and seller partners in the eternal ritual of a transfer of property is not a form of ingratiation even by a delicate person's book. For it does not pretend to represent more than it actually contains: style, ceremony, an embodiment in the flesh of the spirit of commerce. A ritual spectacle without which the market loses its charm and its flavor.

Immediately after the battle in Old Jerusalem appeared a few stalls selling cold beverages. Boys collected from somewhere an ammunition crate, placed in it a block of ice, and laid on top of it a row of bottles filled with beverages of powerful colors to delight the eye. The dust had not yet settled on the ruins, but the debilitating heat of summer bred a torrid thirst. By its very nature this encounter of supply and demand contained in it a gesture of politeness and a sense of the unity of contrasts. The need to sell and the urge to buy greeted, embraced each other. As in the saw of the cow and the calf: More than the one wished to slake his thirst the other desired to provide the beverage.

The next day the steel shutters rose from in front of the haberdashery stores and let the eye glean their colorful treasures. Stalls were set up near the en-

Jerusalem, Mount Zion

trances—minute agencies of temptation to those rushing by—and merchants stood by them with the sugared countenance of philanthropists wishing to confer their bounty upon others. It was not much longer before the whole market stirred, rose to life, and spread far and wide its fragrance, uproar, and delight.

During the first days we still walked about the market armed, not certain we could trust that fraternization of buyers and sellers that ceases the moment an article has changed hands in return for cash. There were also many who feared that these marks of peace were no more than a mask. But the double column of traders standing each by the entrance of his tiny store along the street with the mercantile smile on his face made our weapons redundant and slightly ludicrous. So, fairly shortly we rid ourselves of all excess burdens and took it upon ourselves instead to observe the laws of the market.

Without a measure of cordiality one cannot sell even essentials, let alone luxuries. The smile here glows with greater power still than the glitter of the very product that would attract to itself a love on first sight.

My part is not with them who believe the market-smile wholly a lie, a gilded wrapper of spoiled merchandise. It suffices you to look at the face of your enemy of yesterday, who but a few days ago joined the screams of an ecstatic mob and who sung invigorating songs of war till hoarse, for you to feel that the embarrassed smile on his chafed lips as he stands there commending to your attention a basketful of figs does not occur on the surface only. You may have no part in it, but his smile, that makes you a partner in the concern for the future of a kilo of almonds, is born of dumb reflection on the enormity of the might of the market. A philosophy of existence presents you its physical representation in a smile, acknowledges the justice of the market's judgment, admits the customer's right to exist—the-customer-is-always-right— prays for peace in the manner of merchants who cannot do without laws of cash, freedom from fear, open highways, insurance, open markets, and a strife of peaceful coexistence between money and merchandise, buyers and sellers. Whenever they present a watermelon, an aubergine, or a clutch of pencils they bow their heads to the need to produce and sell, and smile shamefacedly in memory of their greedy dream: to take by force.

Even if you stroll about just to look and have no intention to buy you are still a part of the market. Even if your pockets are empty and your hand does not feel the tomatoes, the nylon pajamas, the olives, the apples, and the charcoal-blackened brass utensils, you still participate in the endless process of buying and selling. For your walk for a walk's sake and your natural curiosity urge others to buy. When your fellow gives in to his desire to possess, he feels as if he followed the example of the others.

There are some markets that are clearly defined: from there to here a market, from here to there tranquil dwellings. However, since the war has been over, it seems that all bounds have exploded, every square is a market place and trading stalls have appeared suddenly in each and every historic site. Every idler has turned into an idle trader and every child free of school, the proud owner of an icebox; there is not a scrap of shade but a seller's fruit basket squeezes into it, and each tree by the roadside has become an open-air store; every car breakdown on the Jenin-Hebron road immediately attracts to its environs a dozen mercantile volunteers; and every road bend, steep incline, each place where age-weary engines tire, witnesses the improvisation of a fruit and cold-drinks stall; and after a day or two, when the old stocks are exhausted, it dresses up in the latest and brightest of Jewish posters. All roads leading to Jerusalem are markets. Some are markets open to all trades—side by side they sell kebab and children's footwear, seductive nightgowns and school copybooks, waxes and rusted keys, horseshoes and TV sets, za'atar and patent medicines for diarrhea, tobacco leaves and ritual utensils, flour and coal, cheeses and perfumes—a vertiginous jumble of colors, smells, and sounds. Through it all, man and donkey walk, treating merchandise with a pinching hand or a skeptic muzzle. Housewives are torn between secret cravings and their capacity to carry.

Some markets are restricted. There only one kind of merchandise is sold. As in the perfume market and butchers' market of the Old City. The one cannot stand the smell of the other, and they have neither of them a need of purchasers who do not come there for the explicit purpose of buying. They respect only those who know their own minds. They dislike it when demand is aroused by touching. Utter aristocrats! They are quiet markets, these, where wares

are not vocally described, where merchants do not await a buyer on the threshold of their stores. They sit inside by their desks, and they do not rush their patrons either. Although they are numerous and neighboring to one another, they do not fear competition. Apparently they make, not lose money on one another. These are markets with a market tradition of world renown, and they would never trade it for ephemeral market bustle.

It seems that many in the mountains of Hebron and Judea found fault in the purchasing habits of the markets' conquerors. Those used to supermarkets did not adapt with ease to the manners of the oriental bazaar and were enticed into buying goods they had no need of. And since they had not been experienced in the grandiloquent encomium accorded in oriental markets even to rotting fruit, many made fools of themselves. Nevertheless and after the fact, their acts have caused much good. By putting Israeli coins in a boy's palm, in spite of the paper bag which swiftly wrapped up beautiful apples that lay atop their spoiled brethren, they put in the boy's hand a kernel of peace. Even had this boy escaped then to a corner, there to sneer at their innocence—that although they were older they lacked experience and knew not the ways of the market—a seed of wisdom had been sewn in his mind. For although he outwitted them he cannot forget that their likes have come out of the war victorious. And perhaps from there shall enter him a seed of doubt: that perhaps petty tricks and cunning knavery are not the sole basis of the world.

But even if all this be but the swish of the tail of a white ass we saw in a dream, and all that had occurred during that swift process of "trade relations" was the placing of Israeli coins in a hand that formerly had sought dinars, only that and nothing nobler, even then we are compelled to admit that that tiny mite too is worth something. A boy who was taught in school that the future belongs to the violent who shall grab their rights by force, learns here in the market improvised under a blazing sun that even the sale of a half kilo of green cucumbers is a matter for negotiations.

THE TOWN OF NAZARETH.

CHRISTIANITY IN THE STREETS.

In Jericho, Bethlehem, Jerusalem, and Tiberias it would crouch behind lock and key. Beneath its turrets and crosses, its chill irons, the mountainous echo of its bells, behind the high walls, the tree-crowded gardens, Christianity used to present to us, natives of Israel, its festive hush, the music of its ritual, the modest-deliberate walk of its priests and monks that are removed from our world in all they can be, as some secret shared by an underground

128

Christmas
in Bethlehem (1967)

Nazareth

movement that has an estate all its own. In Nazareth it was wild in the streets. Here it was sold wholesale and to private buyers too.

But precisely here, not as in the monasteries in Judea's desert and in the plains of the Dead Sea, its revelation had failed to confer even a shadow of inspiration on the streets and markets. In our eyes it was an Arabic town. A district city that housed government offices one cannot do without and that therefore one went to on secular pilgrimage, incidentally also to enjoy some oriental cooking and coffee prepared with "hel."

Nazareth was a market, workshops, and government offices. Guests of other nations we took to the crib of their faith. On the threshold of the church we observed on their faces an instant of grace, a warming heart-pang of the memory, recalled from distant childhood of happy moments of innocent faith, a kneeling prayer by the side of the bed and the Christmas tree that promises delightful surprises. The official guide, under the British as under the Israeli authorities—he is probably the same fellow, anyway—has already had much experience in guessing the temper of the tourists who wish to look at holy remains packed in glass cases. His voice improvises in many keys and develops one or another in accordance with the glow of grace or the cold glitter of the skeptic, as the case may be, that brightens his listeners' eyes. He has a pathetic melody, as well as scientific formulas that come to terms with the irrational desires of the human heart. He needs once the one, once the other, always the tip. Jews he supplies with historic "information." Dates, facts, guesses unencumbered by the distributor's responsibility; also general data on the architecture of the building and the cost of the golden robes.

130

The street teems with people. A stormy political life and a raucously economic one. The ancient next to the newly born. Sacred souvenirs—ancient stones and stained glass that fell out of a window which previously had scattered an enchanted light on a spectacle of Christian surrender to grace in one of the churches hereabout—are sold off a stall crowding another that sells lambs' meat, fowls' entrails, and jars of brass. The two are rubbing shoulders. The smell of coffee pervades everything, mingled with the stench of sewage that flows here mildly down the incline along the paved watercourse that cleaves the narrow alley in two. Paupers and cripples sit at the market entrance by a new Cadillac decorated with double antennas and vacationing beggars rest outside the coffeehouse looking, between the legs of patrons sitting inside, at a Lebanese TV program that alternates bellydancing with prayers.

Two nuns who are strolling about the market, intent on Monday's shopping, chafe and evade in the general scramble of elbows poking ribs, touch yet not touch all that is offered at full price, half price, and for the taking: goods, bargains, and stolen glances. The one who bought a bright plastic bag is a devotee of the old way; she who has a satchel of woven straw, in the oriental manner, hanging with graceful negligence from her arm is a devotee of the new. For the most modern of moderns are now avid for the straw that Nazareth supplies in plenty.

THE NEW CITY.

This weakness of the moderns is already well known to Nazareth merchants. The price of earthernware jars, brass utensils, and straw baskets rises with every new building built in the new Nazareth that overlooks the old city from its lofty perch. The child with the running nose riding the old donkey at the town entrance plays with a plastic donkey doll. The foreign tourist will reverently pick from the ground slivers and pieces of the old jar he threw down there as useless.

Some come here for the good of their souls, others to fix radiators. A simple visit of God's commissioner in Nazareth adds one dime of wealth to every inhabitant, one Christian, one Moslem, one Jew. Each additional dime is progress. And progress means fewer bazaars and more department stores. Upper new Nazareth no longer depends on the old Nazareth in the valley, and the government offices, too, have climbed up the mountain. The new town is bound in the end to swallow up the old. An office of Public Works of the Federation of Hebrew Labor in Israel builds a new wing to the Church of Annunciation. A tripartite peaceful coexistence of three major religions develops slowly within progressive relationships of trade. The new manner leaves its stamp on all.

Some old customs pass away and some persist. One young Arab, a Christian,

Meiron - Tomb of Rabbi Shimon Bar Jochai

אמרון - קבר/שמעון בר /יוחאי.

a lorry-driver who works "only for Jews," boasted to me that his wife does not do the least stroke of work. His outlook on these things is: either Love or Work. "They don't go together." And since he loves his wife "like a Frenchman" and not "like an Arab" he creates for her "a piece of Paris" in Nazareth. She doesn't do a thing all day except lie on her bed and get fat. Until she becomes really beautiful. If she feels like a glass of water, our young friend's mother must hasten and bring her a glass of water lest the "loving-beloved" tire her own person. The boy works hard and wants, when he returns home, to enjoy himself in this world. A tired love "is not a business" for him. Modern times—modern melodies.

It is already possible to see a husband and wife having a public row in the market place. The woman is no longer terrified of her man's beatings. She wanted to buy some chemical detergents that stand here on the stalls in enticing colored boxes, but her man held that "sand does it better." Since she insisted on buying, he cursed her father and mother. But although he threatened her with raised fists she ignored him, took money from her purse, and bought as she wanted. Seeing her thus rebellious, he threw her a choleric glare and mounted his donkey. The woman collected her parcels, the colored tin can included, and walked behind the donkey, as of old. But something nevertheless has changed. Maybe one day soon the man will get off the donkey or, at least, will spare his wife from carrying the baggage.

134

SAFAD IN AZURE AND PURPLE.

YESTERDAY AND THE DAY BEFORE.

"On the night of Tammuz 12, the fear of God reigned in town; for strange men walked the streets whose faces reflected wrath and evil." So wrote Eliezer Halevy, secretary to Minister Montefiore. "The Rabbi asked me to dispatch a request to the town governor not to leave us in our period of need but to be our protection as was promised by Abdul Hadi. I did as the Rabbi requested. The clerk answered me in the manner of the Arabs and swore by his head and by the light of his eyes that he would protect the town and not budge from it. Nevertheless we knew there was no value to that oath. . . . With rifles, knives, hatchets, and clubs, they beat us and inflicted upon us grievous wounds till blood flowed. Afterwards, they chased us out and perhaps a thousand times waved their swords threateningly above our heads that we tell them the place where we had buried our treasures . . ."

The year 1837 was the year of the quake. "His fury poured like fire and the land heaved and quaked, a very terrible tumult," wrote Menachem Mendel of Kamenitz, the chronicler of *Annals of the Times*. "In the towns of Safad and Tiberias (and not as the rabble believes, that the earth opened up, no, but it moved and trembled as a horse that ripples its skin), and the domes of buildings caved in atop the dwellers whose houses became their graves; and greater still was the ordeal of the houses that were atop the mountains;

135

but whosoever were abroad, nothing bad befell them. Some two-thousand souls died in these two towns and many persons became crippled and suffered terrible agonies and lost extremities and many of the congregation of the Yeshiva died in talit and tfillin . . ."

When I first saw Safad, a hundred years after these events, it appeared to have grown out of the riots and the quake. A minute Jewish congregation sat there in ruined houses, awaiting in talit and tfillin a catastrophe or salvation. A few laymen already sat along the main Jewish street, tradesmen and craftsmen, whose sons, who had prospered, had escaped to Tiberias or Haifa. A brilliant azure sky was spread over the town when we came there on a youth movement trip and when the sun went down, the roofs shone with a dull purple glow. From the eyes of a poor girl, the survivor of woes and misfortune, gleamed a mysterious fear of life. The clang of hobnailed working boots sounded in the ancient alleys of Safad as the marching echo of foreign invaders who wield their terror in each and every generation on this ancient, suffering-trained race. We felt we were not welcomed in Safad: by the Arabs, because they saw in our confident upright mien a challenge to their mastery; by the Jews, because our festive secularism—an impertinence towards the heavens, our love of land and love of life but minus the mysteries—presented a manner of settling the country they had wanted no part of. Later, during the War of Independence, an alliance was formed between them and us. The cannon of the Palestine salvation army that had been placed in Meron

Safad
"Ha-Ari" Synagogue

Safed

breached the ancient walls of Jewish Safad and dug craters in the orchards, but bridged the abyss that lay between us and them. In the days of the martial law of the Palmach boys they appended a crown of reverence and a halo of spiritual glow to those secular affairs that were conducted there with the same courage and purity that the communal life of the "recruited Hachshara" fostered as sacred principles. They obeyed the orders of the Governor, aged twenty-two, and stood at his chamber's door as Hassids at their Rabbi's court.

On the day Arabic Safad was taken, they went along the streets to see the vengeance as if they had not yet healed the wounds inflicted in 1834 and 1921. Places that do not change their appearance have, it seems, a much deeper historic memory. Ephemeral longings for redemptions in azure and purple had suddenly become stark reality. They who had wielded a sword

over their heads yesterday or a century or two hundred years ago now ran away from them in fear of their lives. Only the next morning did they remember that their joy had been premature. The Messiah had not arrived; merely the trippers of yesterday arrived as conquered. So they returned to the synagogues and went back to collecting charity monies by a ruined building which was said to have been Jacob's baths. And beneath the graceful blue of a tall sky they dug yet once again the trench that had been filled in between the sacred and the profane.

FROM MOUNT CANAAN—A HASTY DRAWING.

But the new Safad burst out and spread. The houses that had been destroyed in the no-man's-land between the quarters relinquished building plots for sale. Where once a fierce battle raged, hand to hand, from house to house, they are building today a hotel or a resthome where it is possible to recuperate in an abstemious fashion: lots of air, a little food, and much change in atmosphere, which sometimes combine to do for a man more, it seems, than simple stuffing and protracted slumbers. But that change-in atmosphere business appears to go and diminish. Ancient Safad is slowly crumbling. New houses are built, the price of land rises, and mystery reservations fall to the ruthless hands of contractors and subcontractors who uncover beneath the Safadic ruins the treasures that have evaded the rioters of the last century. The empty lot is the treasure. And soon there won't be any more ancient

treasures, nor mysteries inside the cool niches of the stone buildings with the pointed vaults. Everything is laid open to the winds and the sun.

The artists, the new inhabitants of Israeli Safad, fear for the future of the ancient city. They had come there after the War of Independence to acquire inspiration wholesale. They had leased abandoned houses—some that were in ruins and some that even the frescoes on their ceilings, in unfashionable taste and of mysterious origin, were still fairly discernible: heart-shaped leaves in blue and purple inside curly necklets of arabesquelike decorations, and similar wall decorations of previous generations. Ancient tastelessness has a charm of its own. The artists have rebuilt the ruins, in the original forms and torn windows facing the azure mountains and purple skies. Beyond they could see the old houses of the inhabitants of Arabic Safad, plastered blue, the fruit gardens of the roofs, the atmosphere of the purifying abste-miousness of poverty, and fears of ancient times that still reign here in the alleys of the ancient town. The fragrance of an ancient source, the warmth of old communality, and the deep sense of the reverence of earth and sky have come to them from the lower city that sparkles in the days of blue but grays in the Galilean rain under a darkling sky.

Now they are trying to save Safad from its innovators. But life has a logic of its own. Safad's earliest inhabitants today walk its alleys as some somber reservation of a past that is viewed with astonishment by modern life, peering at it from store display windows of electronic products and canned delicacies. A reservation of the past, but one not hedged, nor nursed with green, with no one to collect entrance fees at a visitors' gate. Tomorrow there shall be left only the paintings, and that providing the artists will draw Safad as it properly is and not merely as a mood piece in azure and purple.

KINNERET, KINNERET.

At the beginning it was a legend, a symbol, a melody—the birthplace of the original workers' movement in Israel, the gracious, diligent sister of the roaring lion of Tel-Hai, "a pitcher of water, a basket, a rake, thence to distant fields to toil." "Were you real or was I dreaming?" (lengthily, in the longing-suffused voice of a pretty girl in a black sarafan and white shirt), a divine voice of fervor of a meaning as yet unclear, a kind of means of identification with a secular negation that a young man of the Eretz Israel of Labor adopts to himself, the ecstasy behind the backs of black, heaving mules. "A picture on the ledge" of a group of pioneers in wide-brimmed straw hats and pio-neeresses in long white dresses, a world's sorrow at a depth of 200 meters below sea level . . .

From near it was so real, so available that the body desired to be swept into it in a more entire connection. "Distant fields!" When all is so near and

140

At the Tomb of Rabbi Shimon bar Yohai, in the Upper Galilee

Tiberias

enclosed, here the water and here the mountain's wall . . . and so familiar!
And the Tel Aviv child saw in it only two things new: all his life he knew a
sun set at sea and now he saw it rising shining on the water; and a blue that
has a limit. For until that day the azure was a matter of infinity—sea, skies,
and whatever goes far to the distance drawing traces of blue in its wake—
and now it is bounded by a bank across. And so it seems as if the blue is captive, securely tight, not to escape again.

And that is the reason for her being so near to heart and explicitly earthy,
and marvelously beautiful and desired as a place to live in even in poverty
and anguish. Something that used to try and escape got caught. Something
ephemeral has put its feet into boots caked in mud. And when you dipped,
the sweetness of the water that you could drink while bathing was a perfection
made whole, a harmony incorporated. All the virtues of water in one. And
in the shade of the bushes by the head of Jordan, you could feel with un-
believable pleasure a cool warmth and a dry dampness—the materialization
of an abstraction. Kinneret, Kinneret . . .

HAIFA FROM THE WEST TO THE EAST.

Once, when flying was still the privilege of a rarefied few who yet had already begun to go abroad, it was Haifa that welcomed us upon our return. Nor, indeed, is return by sea at all similar to the descent of an airplane in an airfield in the middle of the country. A person coming by air takes his lunch in London—a gelid solemnity, the chill of frost and haughty demeanor, roast and prunes, *Evening News,* a snowbound street and driving on the left of the road—and his evening meal here under a clear sky. Here are the lights, the whisper of wheels on runway, there the relatives on the terrace, and in a few minutes he is already on this side of the fence, in Hebrew, in coins which are not foreign, on the right of the road and hot in his coat, and as of now whatever occurs in London is again relegated to the stature of foreign news. And suddenly it seems that all this business of homesickness is perhaps a trifle exaggerated. Demonstrably Israel is not all that far. Nor is America. Africa likewise. The empty wallet alone makes distances distances. The affluent have a small world. It seems they have lost their right to be homesick when abroad, for they can easily climb up the gangway and into an airplane that brings them within forty winks to a place where they speak their language and understand their ills. Between twilight and nightfall they are able to quiet that heart-pinching agitation by a flying glance at their childhood's province before they return to their occupations abroad.

He who comes by sea is not like them. He has leisure to pry into sentiments and to reach the essential substance of the return to the homeland. Abroad, until the boat casts its moorings, he can look at length at that life going on below, other men's lives that he had wished to peer into, understanding but one part in three, and that would now continue along without him,

without sorrowing at his departure, without at all missing him. And by the time the ship has left the harbor he can cut loose, without any fuss, that thread of fraternization that connected him to a place not his own and to good men who are not his brothers in fortune. The forms on the beach dwarf and diminish, their lines becoming once more foreign and obscure, and the fishing vessels making their way to their home port appear to travel in an opposite direction. And in a short while the port town is but a picture post-card of itself, and a while later it is mist or a glow at the foot of distant hills that in a while longer shall become a nimbus of clouds in the horizon. After that he has very much leisure to lie on his back on deck, eyes fixed on the tall blue now that they have tired of the deep blue, and to meditate the antic-ipated meeting with family and home, the burning eyes of the children behind the customs' barrier, the delighted welcome of friends, the look of his own room that is filled by his presence and emptied by his absence, and to wonder about the slow progression of the time that yet did not allow sunset longer than a bare few minutes. There is leisure, too, to form friendships with new people who are subjects of the same fortune.

And there is time to look a lengthy hour at that perpetual motion towards

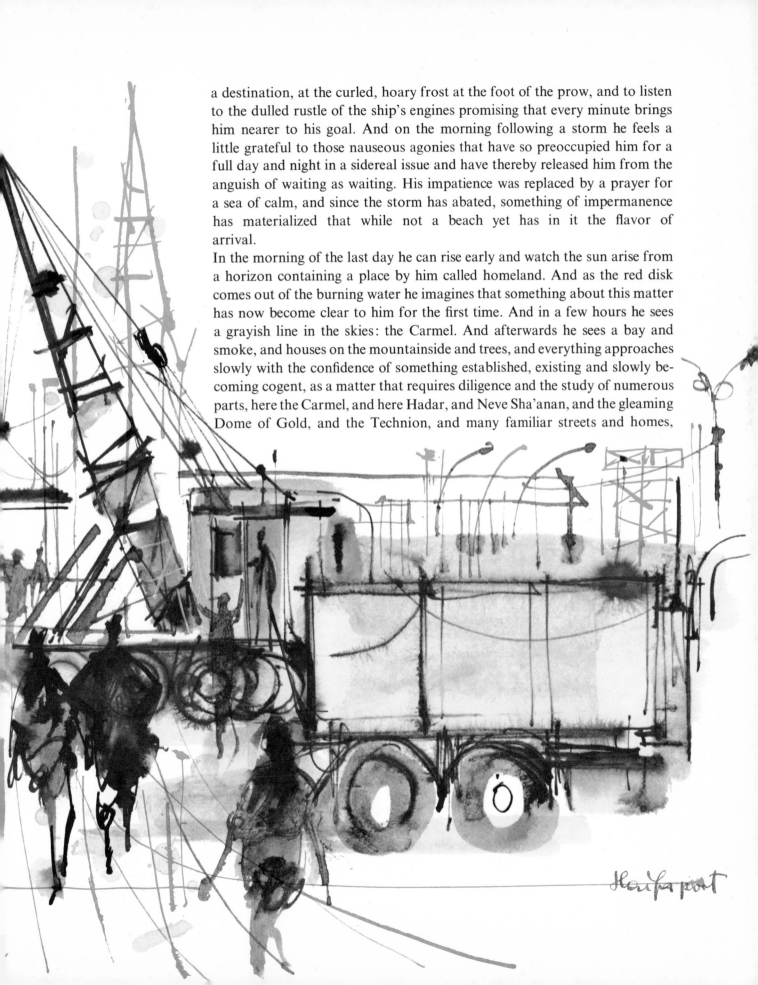

a destination, at the curled, hoary frost at the foot of the prow, and to listen to the dulled rustle of the ship's engines promising that every minute brings him nearer to his goal. And on the morning following a storm he feels a little grateful to those nauseous agonies that have so preoccupied him for a full day and night in a sidereal issue and have thereby released him from the anguish of waiting as waiting. His impatience was replaced by a prayer for a sea of calm, and since the storm has abated, something of impermanence has materialized that while not a beach yet has in it the flavor of arrival.

In the morning of the last day he can rise early and watch the sun arise from a horizon containing a place by him called homeland. And as the red disk comes out of the burning water he imagines that something about this matter has now become clear to him for the first time. And in a few hours he sees a grayish line in the skies: the Carmel. And afterwards he sees a bay and smoke, and houses on the mountainside and trees, and everything approaches slowly with the confidence of something established, existing and slowly becoming cogent, as a matter that requires diligence and the study of numerous parts, here the Carmel, and here Hadar, and Neve Sha'anan, and the gleaming Dome of Gold, and the Technion, and many familiar streets and homes, and there buses that leave Haifa and go to his home. And while the officials worry with the tourists, he has leisure to stand on deck and to cast to his relatives shouts that drown in the shouts of others who stand beside him and act in a similar manner. But there is nothing to it. Each picks from the general uproar and adopts to himself a melodious tone that is meant for him. Homeland.

And when all the formalities are done with, again he is on this side of the fence, among his family. And Haifa is as it has always been, a city he remembers from his childhood, a gate to the far-away, a doorway to distant longings, a city in which every window opens on to mountain and sea, a city of rising chimneys and forests of pine, and which has in it one part of sixty of abroad, for the sun that goes down in its sea shall never catch up with a vessel going far away along that path of gold that it throws from horizon to shore.

THE KIBBUTZ.

A GENERAL IMPRESSION.

A visitor who comes to Israel wants to see the kibbutz. In a new place he wants to see that which he does not have at home. Every Israeli is connected with the kibbutz in one way or another even if he has set foot in one only by sheer accident. Many cleared a field of stones and departed before sowing; sowed but did not bring in the harvest; dug a foundation but did not build a wall; sat under their roofs but did not see children surround them. Some saw their sons go there and some wondered to themselves why they, too, had not gone to field and furrow, to the border and to the great campaign. And since there is in the kibbutz attachment among people that has much mutual trust in it, the lives of all others, whether they want it or not, are weighed against that measure. Men of faith, looking out at life from their own corner of it, inquire into the quality of the kibbutz's faith. Those who have little faith cannot believe the kibbutz is what it looks like. Neither kind treat it as just another place where other men live. Sometimes they borrow strength from it, other times they are made happier by finding faults in it. Some find it to enjoy their private reminiscences, now that the kibbutz no longer is as it used to be in their youth, when they dug trenches and burnished guns. And others regret it no longer has the proud poverty of youthful recollections.

More than a kibbutz has members, it has ex-members outside it. Far more numerous are those who came and saw and left. Some—their leaving was done in sorrow. Others—with relief. Yet others—in the urgency of leaving

148

and having it done with. And yet others—following a dialogue of aching hearts and many sleepless nights. Some left in a moment of weakness; and some because the kibbutz wasn't enough mature to solve their problems. Sometimes disrupted relations between individuals removed a one from being one of many. And sometimes—conflicting beliefs which were equally void the next day. Some that left maintain unpretentious ties of friendship. Others cannot overcome the disappointment that keeps gnawing their hearts away. Some keep a distance, out of refinement of sensibilities; and some, by stout friendship, remained "within the family." There is the one who has left and forgotten—as one who, having moved house from one address to another, remembers merely a scrap of view, a tree, a running brook, and bushes in whose privacy love had transpired. And there is the one who left and whose entire life became a wandering over a withered soul.

Arriving at a kibbutz's yard, one has not arrived at a given place of such and such a name. He has come to the kibbutz. And he feels it the moment he sets his foot inside the gate. And because he is at a place in which exists a particular form of communal life, this fact is reflected in everything that his eyes alight upon: a man's laughter, the talk of young boys, the prettiness of cattle, the color of the green, the rustle in the trees, and the countenance of whoever met him and asked to aid his purpose.

Our journey cannot stop at one kibbutz and skip the others, for they all deserve attention. At first sight they appear most similar to one another. But for a person experienced in such, it suffices to look at the main yard, to peer into a member's room, to study the face of the crowd as it gathers, to find out how very different they are, the one from the others. This one, the agricultural existence has left its marks upon. The other—its poverty is steeped in joy and contained pride. That one—its sons are its secret strength. And that—its young generation is its secret woe. The one has a good soil but a somber countenance; the other has a look of delight though an ungrateful soil. One has both the one and the other—a beautiful farm and a civilized culture—while its neighbor is conspicuously lacking in both.

Nor are the young kibbutzim like the veteran ones. The new—their lives are still an adventure, although they are wholly involved with the here-and-now and are enthusiastically busy with material preoccupations. The veterans slowly progress along their life of three generations, hoping to transmit from generation to generation that revolutionary ardor and the sense of Jewish pride that lit a blaze in Europe at the turn of the century. Nor are those kibbutzim whose private quarters are well maintained yet whose general aspect is neglected similar to kibbutzim that indulge in conspicuous public display and keep spartan private quarters.

A kibbutz cannot allow itself to be old, for its life is so conducted that each and every generation can cast doubts on that which does not enjoy the ap-

149

proval of the times. Nor can it be young, for the young and vigorous are called to assume responsibilities before they have even admitted them. The elders cannot say "I have done my share," and the young cannot say "In time I shall do my part"—forever their kibbutz hungers for their toil. Yet it has no manner of compelling its members to produce their day's worth except in the sympathy it gives them in return for their loyalty. It has no means of payment except that which is unspoken—a reflection in the eye; nor has it punishments to mete except that which is covert in the looks of others. There are neither rewards nor punishments. The simple weakness of others is here the transgression of an unwritten law. Intellectual work must be vital to justify its existence when a man's peers are steeped in material affairs that are inescapable. Deadening services can become a manner of attachment to others if a love of others be present in their execution.

Therefore we have said: We shall write only that which can be found in all kibbutzim. An anonymous kibbutz. Singular and peculiar yet like another, common and rare. A one that is general and many, that we have seen in its thousand aspects: in its labor—that which has a virile glory, at the heights of gigantic machines, and which is needed in its time and which increases a man's measure who does not evade it, such as cleaning out the sewer in the communal kitchen; at a meeting of the many in a general assembly, where matters both great and small are decided in a supposedly democratic manner; when silently, dexterously, it takes the infants down to the shelters; when it discovers new aspects in its members when with guns they face a threatening wood; in a fervent run against burning fields; in a general mobilization to gather under roofs hay that stands bare in danger of rain; in demented uproar on the sport field; in a secret dialogue with a member who has slipped; in the tired faces that make effort to listen at a lecture on literature; in the sprawl of parents and children on green lawns, by birds and water sprinklers; in the overt and covert pride of parents watching a graduation show at the school; in a moment of weakness, envy, help-lessness, lessening; in the fraternization called into being by the need to defend a defeated; in all that is of it and in it, within it and on its fringes, at the foundation, atop the crown, and in what emanates from it, intangible.

And so we chose to describe one hour of night far from the place in which the essence of the matter has its being.

NOCTURNAL RECONNAISSANCE IN A KIBBUTZ.

Night. In the dining room the kibbutz is celebrating an anniversary. A third, fourth, or fifth decade's. There is a tumult of revelers, a clatter of cutlery, and sounds of laughter. The distant past is recalled and revived with affection. Whether mules and horses be allowed in the dining room, and the goats'

152

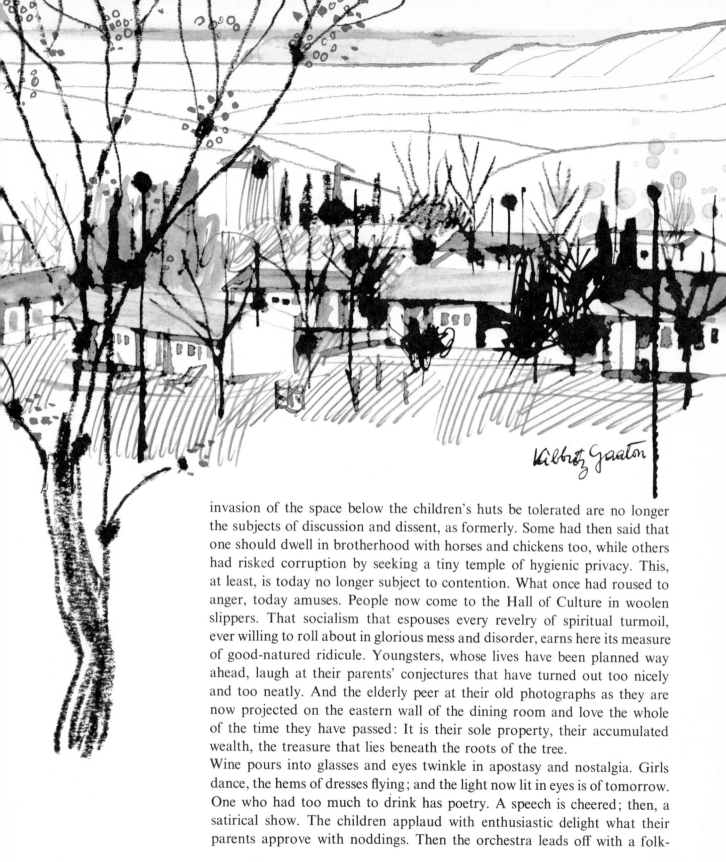

invasion of the space below the children's huts be tolerated are no longer
the subjects of discussion and dissent, as formerly. Some had then said that
one should dwell in brotherhood with horses and chickens too, while others
had risked corruption by seeking a tiny temple of hygienic privacy. This,
at least, is today no longer subject to contention. What once had roused to
anger, today amuses. People now come to the Hall of Culture in woolen
slippers. That socialism that espouses every revelry of spiritual turmoil,
ever willing to roll about in glorious mess and disorder, earns here its measure
of good-natured ridicule. Youngsters, whose lives have been planned way
ahead, laugh at their parents' conjectures that have turned out too nicely
and too neatly. And the elderly peer at their old photographs as they are
now projected on the eastern wall of the dining room and love the whole
of the time they have passed: It is their sole property, their accumulated
wealth, the treasure that lies beneath the roots of the tree.

Wine pours into glasses and eyes twinkle in apostasy and nostalgia. Girls
dance, the hems of dresses flying; and the light now lit in eyes is of tomorrow.
One who had too much to drink has poetry. A speech is cheered; then, a
satirical show. The children applaud with enthusiastic delight what their
parents approve with noddings. Then the orchestra leads off with a folk-

song—a ripened product of a native son just returned from his studies, a rustic beat that has urban knowledge in it and seeks to be likened to the song of the grapes-treader in the winepress. Cowmen whose hands are practiced in automatic milking machines take to heart cowboy songs they have heard on the radio.

The uproar spews through the lighted window as from an incandescent oven. From nearby it is distinguishable in its component sounds: musical instruments, laughter and the rustle that passes through human motion, shifted chairs, crockery and cutlery, the shouted pleadings of the master of ceremonies. Farther from the hall, beyond the first row of houses, it loses its detail. It arrives there as waves of broken moans of laughter. And from there and farther outwards, it is only a fractionated, monotonous susurrus.

Thus it reaches the domain of the children's houses. Here all is tranquil and silent, drenched in deep darkness. The boughs of the carob or the ficus, the poinciana or casuarina shade the lamps that light the paths. Foliage in a disk of light, and the scrap of black skies in it, and the light of a lamp, limited to its pale, cast directly upon the ground, as a desk lamp with its shade pushed low.

A world of stillness. The night nurse, carrying an oil lantern (tomorrow it will be an electric torch; the day after, an electronic toy that sounds even a baby's bleat that the ear cannot hear from far) strolls among the houses. She can't be seen—only her calves and feet are lighted by the weak glow of the lantern's flame. The feet are young or heavy—it cannot be seen from a distance. But as she stops and the lantern sways a minute by her legs, one can sense her listening to the sound of weeping that the night has given birth to. And in an instant she rushes, as some hovering ray of light, into one of the houses. And now her voice is heard from inside one of the sections, a clear motherly voice: "Something is hurting?" A child in a nightgown stands by the entrance. Large eyes widely staring into a night that has no bounds. But a beginning? Middle? End?

"Nothing hurts. But I can't fall asleep. There's noise."

She listens to the dull susurrus from afar. And in a minute she is inside, her hand on the boy's shoulder. Before she leaves, utter silence shall reign there once again.

The wind troubles the limbs of trees over the screen of light. She returns to stroll with the lantern swaying by her legs. A cow's moo breaks through suddenly as if it were a part of the obscure echo that reaches her from the dining room. And then it seems as if in that slight whisper or in the utter silence the festival is contained in its entirety. Shortly her friend will come and take this lamp from her, and then she will go towards the increasing noise. And her friend shall sit on the steps of the children's house with the silence ringing in her ears. A moment of inspiration. Celebration.

154

Mount Hermon
(Golan Heights)

A LOOK AT RAMAT HAGOLAN.

Under the government of Free France, following upon the occupation of Syria by the British, we were detained there, during a hike of the youth movement, on charge of having crossed the border illegally by the Banias. We sat for a few hours at a police station that was too small to hold all of us until the secretary of a neighboring kibbutz arrived, the sound of whose scolding frightened the authority—he flourished a whistling riding crop, as befitting an authority that brooks no arguments, and our liberty was soon restored to us.

A dip that we dipped in a spring of the Banias in 1967 was, therefore, a second dip. And it was suffused with a powerful emotion that this book of ours shall pass over in deep reverence; other books shall take it up most gently and, probably, it shall continue for many days to gleam from dry battle reports, snippets of testimony and reminiscences of others.

We never saw the Golan Heights except from the top of Mount Hermon many years ago. We were sitting on the peak at 2,840 meters, our hearts bursting with pride and joy: our hearts' desire at age seventeen materialized

156

Hammat Gader

at eighteen. We looked down upon the Golan Heights. Our feet drummed the concrete pillar and the map spread out on our knees struggled desperately with the wind. Even the voice we wanted to sound to one another was snatched from us, literally at our mouths, and thrown by the savage wind into the stormy air that faced us and, that to the inhabitants of Damascus, constituted the sky. We had no option but to look and keep silent. The snow was burning in the twilight below us, and Damascus was sinking into tremulous darkness among its gardens and orchards.

We watched the Golan Heights with great pity. So poor it was in flora, in comparison with the fertile Hula Valley. We charged it to the debit of its nature: a Godforsaken country that extinguished, extinct volcano craters close upon all sides. Because it was mired in an ancient terror of natural catastrophes, it abstained from settling the land. Or so it used to look, from above.

So it looks now, too, from near, abstaining from settling the land. But not so much because of its nature as because of the terror it sought to strike in the hearts of its neighbors. A land of advanced fortifications and primitive agriculture. Cannons and donkeys. Florid expostulations and rabid illiteracy. A sad story of villages without village smells, a soil drenched with gun oil, and farmers who sow mines. A land that is praying for true farmers and peace.

STOP! BORDER AHEAD!

At the back of the north, on the road to Damascus and on every road that leads to no-man's-land along Israel's borders, there stand signs in three languages: "Stop! Border ahead!" Far beyond it is possible to discern the frontier posts of Syria. And as you walk there, quite innocently, you never know how far the finger across the border is from the trigger.

And we have already grown accustomed to it. And children that live in shelters may grow up here with the consciousness that this is the way of the world and the nature of the place, and that it is easier to shift a torrent from its course and to drain away the water of an inland sea than it is to remove from their lives the gun barrel that ever follows them as they walk in the fields. They have known that the hatred is as fierce as hell and deeper than the deep sea and that many rivers shall not extinguish the flame.

157

Is it indeed a decree of faith from which there is no escape? And the girl with the oil lamp, is she not of the place and the time?

It happened only in 1942. We were walking, four boys, on our way from the top of Hermon to the sources of the Jordan. We had, admittedly, a pistol hidden in the double-bottomed water bottle, but we had not needed it even once. Shepherds we chanced across called us, amongst themselves, "Askar El Yehud," and although they had not mistaken our identities, had seen in us Jewish soldiers and knew that we had stolen across the border, they welcomed us and even gave us as much steaming goats' milk as we could drink, refusing payment.

Darkness fell when we were coming down the ridge. Since we were hurried, we cancelled our original plan to avoid an unexpected encounter with the Free French police by walking along the top of the ridge, and we turned, instead, to a path that passes through a village situated in a mountain break that cannot be bypassed. We intended to slip through the village orchards under the cover of dark. Farther along, the road was open to slip unseen back into Israel. Nevertheless, we ran into strangers. In the narrow road, through which water flowed so that to pass it we had to skip from stone to stone, we met two strangers. They informed us the police were in the village and that we should hide. They said and they did. They took us to their home and sheltered us under their own roof. They served us fruit and drink, and sat down to figure out how to transport us through the danger zone. A solution was found.

A girl of twelve, carrying an oil lamp, led us among the orchards, along a track used by smugglers. And so she led us in silence a long way until we saw the lights of our homeland beyond. An Arab girl alone with four foreign men. At night. Far from human habitation. On a deserted mountain path. Without any fear. By her father's bidding.

She received our farewells with a bow of the head and then returned to her father's house. First a girl, then a lighted silhouette, and later still a tiny flame in the mountain heights.

And we went running down to the fields by the foothills of the mountain.

Peace is not a fairy tale.

Banias, in the Golan